Praise for Becca's
Badass Advice

"Close this book and go start loving now. Risk it, because as we wild women know, life itself is love itself."
—Marni Kamins, author of *The Breakup Repair Kit* and *The Dating Repair Kit*

"This book is essential reading; it's the Bible of Badassery."
—Varla Ventura, author of *Sheroes*

"As any woman of experience can tell you, great advice from a fellow wild woman can be much more than catchphrases. These bold bon mots are a solid roadmap for living a full life. The wise words spoken by these icons of literature, history, comedy, and drama will teach you that you can always get what you want, providing you listen closely."
—Nina Lesowitz, author of *The Party Girl Cookbook*

"You'll be laughing out loud as you learn from these bold, brave women!"
—Louise Harmon, author of *Happiness A to Z*

"Ah, love, luv, *l'amour*! Becca Anderson supplies us with a goodly list of apt quotes from outrageous outspoken women on our favorite subject, interspersed with info bites about women and love. Buy this for your honey, and read it in bed with him/her. That's *amore*!"

—Trina Robbins, author of *Eternally Bad*, *Tender Murderers*, and *Wild Irish Roses*

BADASS ADVICE

Also by Becca Anderson

Badass Affirmations
The Book of Awesome Women
The Book of Awesome Black Women
The Book of Awesome Girls
The Book of Awesome Women Writers
The Joy of Self-Care
Positively Badass
Friendship Isn't a Big Thing, It's a Million Little Things
Affirm Your Life
I Can Do Anything
Female, Gifted, and Black

BADASS ADVICE

Love, Life and Being True to Yourself

Becca Anderson

with A. Leslie Noble

Published by Mango Publishing, a division of Mango Publishing Group, Inc.

Cover, Layout & Design: Morgane Leoni

For permission requests, please contact the publisher at:
Mango Publishing Group
2850 S Douglas Road, 2nd Floor
Coral Gables, FL 33134 USA
info@mango.bz

For special orders, quantity sales, course adoptions and corporate sales, please email the publisher at sales@mango.bz. For trade and wholesale sales, please contact Ingram Publisher Services at customer.service@ingramcontent.com or +1.800.509.4887.

Badass Advice: Love, Life and Being True to Yourself

Library of Congress Cataloging
ISBN: (p) 978-1-68481-102-1 (e) 978-1-68481-103-8
Library of Congress Control Number: 2022946594
BISAC category code SEL035000, SELF-HELP / Self-Management /
Time Management

Printed in the United States of America

To all my gal pals, BFF's and women friends. I have laughed, loved, and learned so much from you, and am very lucky to have you in my life. xoxo

Contents

FOREWORD

I've never met her in person, but I am a huge fan of Becca Anderson. She's written dozens of books and countless articles that help us live more mindful, grateful, courageous, happy, fearless, and wonder-filled lives.

Her audacious, enlivened spirit is palpable and jumps off the pages of her books—most notably, in her latest book, the one that you hold in your hands: *Badass Advice: Love, Life and Being True to Yourself.*

Quite simply, Becca helps us live bolder and better lives.

You may be familiar with a list called the "Top Five Regrets of the Dying," compiled by hospice nurse Bronnie Ware. The first regret on that list is, "I wish I'd had the courage to live a life true to myself, not the life others expected of me."

So many people spend their lives trying to meet familial and cultural expectations. They strive to fit in and not create waves. They repress their owns whims and desires in order to make others happy. And, in the end when it is too late, they fervently wish they had listened to the unique whispers of their spirits.

One of the saddest things in life, I feel, is to sacrifice our own one-of-a-kind, creative expression in order to fulfill cookie-cutter expectations of who we think we should be.

I don't know if Becca is familiar with Bronnie and these common regrets, but this beloved author definitely seems to be on a mission to help people—women, especially!—avoid that big end-of-life regret!

The book you are about to read is a big juicy antidote to regret that will leave you feeling as if your own personal map to authenticity and boldness is in your back pocket.

Chances are, if you chose this book, you are someone on a quest to shed the shoulds and live a zesty life of badassery, architected **just** for you.

The pages of this book are filled with stories and quotes about love, lust, and living a daring life.

Here's what you can expect: awesome advice from amazing women from all walks of life. These authors, actresses, activists, comedians, musicians, philosophers, psychotherapists, and philanthropists offer straight-up, laugh-out-loud, no holds barred guidance on how you can stop squeaking by in a mousy way and start to roar like a lioness!

Between the bios and quotations are some super witty reflections from Becca herself. To whet your appetite, I give you a small taste here:

> *But as life teaches us year after year, it isn't the pedicures, the highlights, or the Spanx that make us beautiful: it's confidence. If you feel your best wearing lipstick and mascara, rock it—you look beautiful. If you prefer patchouli to perfume, own that aroma and be your best self. You see, the secret to being beautiful lies in knowing you always are. After all, confidence is the best accessory a girl can have.*
>
> *In this chapter, you will find quotes from badass women who know that they are beautiful, no matter what society, peers, or parents say.*

You can't hear me, but I'm saying an enthusiastic, absolutely-in-agreement, fist-in-the-air, **yes**!

Maybe the heart of this book is best exemplified in a quote I found, excerpted from one of the many fascinating short bios of badass women: this one from Adalynn (Jonnie) Jonckowski:

"Any time you have the freedom to do what you want to do and exercise that freedom, you're a champ."

Becca Anderson gives us this book as a big ole permission slip to USE the freedom we have in our lives to live and love fully. She's a champ! And she teaches us all how to feel like—and **live** like—champions of our own lives.

Whaddaya waiting for? Turn the page, soak up all this sassiness, and start living out loud! The world desperately needs your brand of baddassery!

—Sherry Richert Belul, author of *Say It Now* and founder of Simply Celebrate

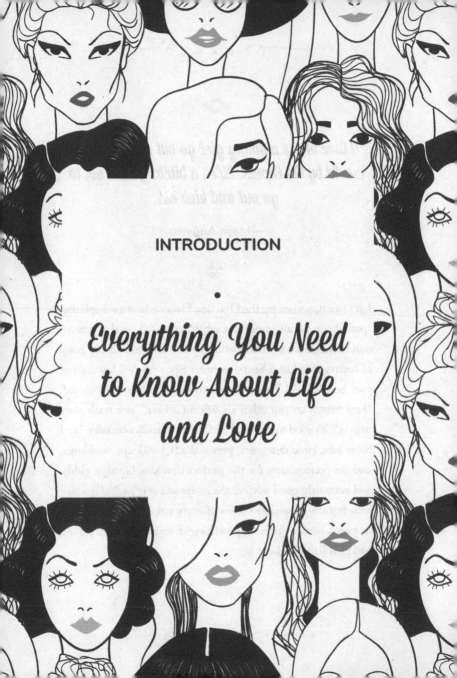

INTRODUCTION

•

Everything You Need to Know About Life and Love

I love to see a young girl go out and grab the world by the lapels. Life's a bitch. You've got to go out and kick ass.

—Maya Angelou

Let's face it, women are the Oral Sex. Here we have a sidesplitting spotlight on the all-important subject of *amore*—and as it turns out, women have a whole lot to say about love. This big book of badassery is like a heart-to-heart talk with two hundred of your best friends! Topics discussed include "love is fabulous," "how friends are our other significant others," "size really does matter," "it's good to get lost," and "are men really necessary?" and cover jobs, blind dates, sex, personal ads, break ups, weddings, and the prerequisites for the perfect first kiss. Gossipy, giddy, and extremely good advice, *this compendium of radical common sense* features loquacious ladies of every stripe from movie stars to moms, literati, glitterati, psychologist, sexperts, and all around bad girls tellin' it like it is.

Growing up, girls are often taught to find a balance between confidence and modesty. Sure, you can accept a compliment, but don't go looking for one. Suggesting that someone look at you would be entirely unacceptable—that girl would be seen as having an ego problem. But all this standard does is make girls question themselves and their own actions left and right. It makes us focus on not emphasizing our attributes when that's really all we should be doing. We don't question this growing up. When our mothers say not to wear that attention-grabbing outfit, or when they criticize us for making a scene, it seems normal and ordinary.

Yet why, I now wonder, in a world where the wind can so easily be knocked out of a woman's sails (whether deliberately and cruelly, or just by the sheer impersonal weight of accumulated experience), would we strive to diet down young girls' egos? Wouldn't it make more sense to shore them up to the size of Kim K's celebrated booty, so that they'd still retain a little buoyancy (a modicum of *oomph!*) despite the inevitable deflationary effects of life?

Happily, the parents of the outspoken badass women in this section seem to have been spectacularly enlightened…or, perhaps, merely spectacularly unsuccessful at inculcating the creed of mouse-like behavior in their daughters. These women never allowed knock-downs to their confidence—they were badass, and they knew it. For amplification of your own sassy attitude—or perhaps just your own amusement—read on.

CHAPTER 1

•

Love Is All You Need. Really?

If there's one thing that's been on the minds of all badass women for as long as we've been around, it's love. And since wild women have been on the scene right from the very beginning, it's safe to say that we've accumulated a veritable stockpile of wit and wisdom on the subject of *amour*—both good and bad. Whether the topic at hand is true love, lost love, scandalous love, or even (heaven forbid) unrequited love, we've always got a good story or an inspiring motto to share.

What better way to celebrate our past, present, and future than with a book devoted to one of our favorite subjects? There are as many kinds of wild love out there as there are wild women, and that's certainly something worth honoring. With this in mind, there's much more to this book than your usual Valentine's card sentiments (although there's plenty of that for you true romantics to enjoy). In the chapter that follows, you'll find reflections on everything from the joys of new love to the heartbreak of divorce, and from lust and sex to loving someone of the same gender. It's all part of what makes us so wonderfully wild, and it's all part of this book as well.

So whether you're in the middle of a lasting romance, starting something new, or even recovering from your last tangle with Cupid's arrows, there's a quote here that will speak to you.

And with legends and life stories of some of the most famous amorous women included in each chapter, you'll be inspired as well as entertained. Love has always been a part of our lives; keep embracing its wildness and add your own stories to those that have come before!

Each of us is born with a box of matches inside us, but we can't strike them all by ourselves.

—**Laura Esquivel,** Like Water for Chocolate

If they substituted the word "Lust" for "Love" in the popular songs, it would come nearer the truth.

—**Sylvia Plath,** The Unabridged Journals of Sylvia Plath

The young habitually mistake lust for love, they're infested with idealism of all kinds.

—**Margaret Atwood,** The Blind Assassin

Love recognizes no barriers. It jumps hurdles, leaps fences, penetrates walls to arrive at its destination full of hope.

—**Maya Angelou,** distinguished poet, memoirist, and civil rights activist

Lust is what keeps you wanting to do it even when you have no desire to be with each other. Love is what makes you want to be with each other even when you have no desire to do it.

—**Judith Viorst,** journalist and psychoanalytic researcher

Lust is temporary, romance can be nice, but love is the most important thing of all. Because without love, lust and romance will always be short-lived.

—**Danielle Steel,** bestselling author

I have not changed; I am still the same girl I was fifty years ago and the same young woman I was in the seventies. I still lust for life, I am still ferociously independent, I still crave justice, and I still fall madly in love easily.

—**Isabel Allende,** noted Chilean-American "magic realism" author

You never lose by loving. You always lose by holding back.

—**Barbara De Angelis,** author and transformational teacher

Love comes when manipulation stops; when you think more about the other person than about his or her reactions to you. When you dare to reveal yourself fully. When you dare to be vulnerable.

—**Dr. Joyce Brothers,** psychologist and columnist

Kiss me and you will see how important I am.

—**Sylvia Plath,** renowned poet and fiction writer

In real love, you want the other person's good. In romantic love, you want the other person.

—**Margaret C. Anderson,** literary magazine founder, editor, and publisher

In our minds, love and lust are really separated. It's hard to find someone that can be kind and you can trust enough to leave your kids with, and isn't afraid to throw her man up against the wall and lick him from head to toe.

—**Tori Amos,** radically insightful singer-songwriter

Love at first sight is easy to understand; it's when two people have been looking at each other for a lifetime that it becomes a miracle.

—**Amy Bloom,** writer and psychotherapist

There is no substitute for the comfort supplied by the utterly taken-for-granted relationship.

—**Iris Murdoch,** Anglo-Irish novelist and philosopher

The only abnormality is the incapacity to love.

—**Anais Nin,** erotic author extraordinaire

Anyone can be passionate, but it takes real lovers to be silly.

—**Rose Franken,** playwright and author

I'm not good at being alone. Especially at the end of the day when my finances are a mess, my car is falling apart, [and] I can't find my shoes. That's when I need a big strong guy to hold me close, so I can look deep into his eyes and blame him.

—Simone Alexander, funny woman who tells it like it is

Love is the difficult realization that something other than oneself is real.

—Iris Murdoch, Anglo-Irish novelist and philosopher

I have no patience for women who measure and weigh their love like a country doctor dispensing capsules. If a man is worth loving at all, he is worth loving generously, even recklessly.

—**Marie Dressler,** stage and screen actress of the silent film and Depression era

You'll discover that real love is millions of miles past falling in love with anyone or anything. When you make that one effort to feel compassion instead of blame or self-blame, the heart opens again and continues opening.

—**Sara Paddison,** writer on human potential

...Dreaming that love will save us, solve all our problems, or provide a steady state of bliss or security only keeps us stuck in wishful fantasy, undermining the real power of the love—which is to transform us.

—**Bell Hooks,** revolutionary author, feminist, and social activist

Divine Love always has met and always will meet every human need.

—**Mary Baker Eddy,** founder of the Church of Christ, Scientist

The greatest science in the word, in heaven and earth, is love.

—**Mother Teresa,** philanthropic missionary nun

Never let a problem to be solved become more important than a person to be loved.

—**Barbara Johnson,** feminist literary critic, translator, and scholar

Badass Clare Boothe Luce: Luce Cannon

Clare Boothe Luce, "the woman with the serpent's tongue," was the anti-Eleanor Roosevelt, a sort of alternate universe doppelganger who used her razor-sharp wit to oppose while "faintly praising" the First Lady and other unrepentant New Dealers. A virulent Republican and FDR basher, Clare was both a smart and tough cookie, albeit not to everyone's taste. Clare, however, had a wholly unique way of asserting her woman power.

As a young woman, one of her summer jobs during college was dropping feminist tracts out of an airplane for some elderly but unstoppable suffragists. Her next job was writing photo captions for *Vogue*; there, the renowned beauty quickly ascended to the position of managing editor at *Vanity Fair*. She was the first woman to hold this post for the glamour glossy and soon proved she could hold her own with the boys, even managing to be welcomed in to their cigarettes and brandy ritual.

Then she met *Time* and *Fortune* magnate Henry R. Luce, married, and quit the day job to write plays, starting with the stinker *Abide with Me* and then surprising everyone with the all-female *To the Women*, a take-no-prisoners satire of snooty society ladies, which went on to become a very successful movie. Clare became an international cause célèbre with the success of *To the Women*, penning a few more stage plays including *Kiss the Boys Goodbye* before she pulled another switcheroo: war correspondent for *Life* magazine on the battle fronts of Burma, India, and China during the early years of World War II. She even interviewed Madame Chiang Kai-shek and Prime Minister Nehru.

Clare's next incarnation was as a politician, and she went on the stump, dissing FDR, Winston Churchill, and a herd of other such sacred cows. She stunned everyone with her gift for rhetoric of the biting, stinging sort. Her next move was to run for a seat as one of Connecticut's representatives in Congress with a very hawkish platform—her slogan was "Let's Fight a Hard War Instead of a Soft War"—and she campaigned for the rights of women, blacks, and workers. Easily winning a seat, she served for four years and then retired while she was ahead. Clare then took her domestic campaigns abroad, convincing the Italian Prime Minister to give Italian women the vote! Her good relations with Italy garnered a post for Clare as the ambassador to Italy in 1953, becoming the United States' second woman ambassador and the first woman chief of mission to a major European power. In 1953, she was fourth in the Gallup poll of the most admired women in the world.

Clare became the grande dame of the Grand Old Party from the Goldwater sixties until her death of cancer in 1987. Clare will be best remembered for her quick wit and verbal virtuosity. She was absolutely one of a kind; she never luxuriated in her husband's great wealth, but instead worked her behind off for many causes and left a legacy of great strides for women in her wake.

Because I am a woman, I must make unusual efforts to succeed. If I fail, no one will say "She doesn't have what it takes." They will say, "Women don't have what it takes."

—**Clare Boothe Luce,** politician and first U.S. woman in a major post as ambassador

Luce Lips

- From the diary Clare kept her psychedelic-inspired musings in when she and hubby Henry dropped acid in 1960: "Capture green bugs for future reference," "Feel all true paths to glory lead but to the grave," and "The futility of the search to be someone. Do you hear the drum?"

- On Veep Henry Wallace, "His global thinking is, no matter how you slice it, globaloney!"

- On Franklin Delano Roosevelt, "Now, I do not for a moment believe that Mr. Roosevelt is a real dictator. Rather, he is a sort of super-duper, highly cultured political boss."

- On Harry Truman, "A gone goose."

- On Eleanor Roosevelt, "No woman in American history has ever so comforted the distressed or so distressed the comfortable."

- On Mississippi senator Theodore Bilbo, "the high muckamuck in America of that muckiest and most vulgar of all modern pagan cults: racism!"

- On the environment, "I am bewildered by the paradox presented by a nation that can land on the moon, orbit satellites 190 million miles from earth, but can't find a way to rid its own landscape of broken-down automobiles."

Love doesn't just sit there, like a stone; it has to be made, like bread, remade all the time, made new.

—**Ursula K. LeGuin,** prize-winning speculative fiction author and poet

I have never met a person whose greatest need was anything other than real, unconditional love.... There is no mistaking love. You feel it in your heart. It is the common fiber of life, the flame that heats our soul, energizes our spirit, and supplies passion to our lives.

—**Elizabeth Kubler-Ross,** pioneering Swiss-American psychiatrist and writer

As you continue to send out love, the energy returns to you in a regenerating spiral.... As love accumulates, it keeps your system in balance and harmony. Love is the tool, and more love is the end product.

—**Sara Paddison,** writer on human potential

Where there is great love, there are always miracles.

—Willa Cather, award-winning author known for novels about frontier life

Loves conquers all things except poverty and toothache.

—Mae West, memorable actress, comedian, screenwriter, and sex symbol

Love is like pi—natural, irrational, and VERY important.

—Lisa Hoffman, entrepreneur and nerdy wit

Esteem Yourself!

You yourself, as much as anybody in the entire universe, deserve your love and affection.

—**Sharon Salzberg,** best-selling author and
Buddhist teacher

Wanting to be someone else is a waste of the person you are.

—**Marilyn Monroe,** iconic actress and singer

The man who does not value himself cannot
value anything or anyone.

—**Ayn Rand,** in The Virtue of Selfishness: A New
Concept of Egoism

For once, you believed in yourself. You believed
you were beautiful and so did the rest of
the world.

—**Sarah Dessen,** author of Saint Anything

One of the greatest regrets in life is being
what others would want you to be, rather than
being yourself.

—**Shannon L. Alder,** Mormon self-help author

Don't waste your energy trying to change opinions.... Do your thing, and don't care if they like it.

—Tina Fey, actress, SNL comedian, writer, and producer

You're always with yourself, so you might as well enjoy the company.

—Diane Von Furstenberg, Belgian-American fashion designer

To lose confidence in one's body is to lose confidence in oneself.

—Simone de Beauvoir, intellectual, writer, philosopher, and social theorist

I never loved another person the way I loved myself.

—Mae West, memorable actress, comedian, screenwriter, and sex symbol

I am my own experiment. I am my own work of art.

—Madonna, iconic performer

I don't entirely approve of some of the things I have done, or am, or have been. But I'm me. God knows, I'm me.

—Elizabeth Taylor, British-American actress and humanitarian

Self-esteem isn't everything; it's just that there's nothing without it.

—**Gloria Steinem,** journalist, activist, and feminist founder of Ms. Magazine

They are called "SELF-worth" and "SELF-esteem" for a reason...we can't let others decide what we are worth, that is so dangerous! Empower yourself!

—**Jaeda DeWalt,** author of Chasing Desdemona

The beauty of a woman must be seen from in her eyes, because that is the doorway to her heart, the place where love resides.

—**Audrey Hepburn,** piquant actress, dancer, and humanitarian

A charming woman...doesn't follow the crowd. She is herself.

—**Loretta Young,** Oscar-winning actress

Every woman is a queen, and we all have different things to offer

—**Queen Latifah,** royal rap star, actress, talk show host, and TV and record producer

Badass Divinity Oshun: Not Your Grandmother's Love Goddess

Known in Africa as the Mother of the River, Oshun is the Yoruba goddess of love, sensuality, and beauty. Though she is said to have a fierce temper when crossed, she most often uses her powers for the benefit of mankind. During the creation of the world, the blacksmith Ogun became tired of working and abandoned his tasks, retreating into the forest. Oshun entered the woods to draw him out, dancing and beguiling him with her splendor. Ogun was so inspired by her loveliness that he took up his tools with more skill and power than he had ever shown before.

Oshun is also a deity of courage and determination. In ancient times, humankind rebelled against Olodumare, the Lord of Heaven, and refused to serve him. Enraged Olodumare brought a drought upon the earth, and the people were afflicted with famine. Birds were sent to beg for the Lord's forgiveness, but none of them was able to fly high enough to reach his house in the sun. Oshun, in the form of a peacock, was the only one able to complete the journey; but by the time she arrived, her beautiful feathers had been burned black as a vulture's. Moved by her bravery, Olodumare restored her and ended the drought, naming her an honored Messenger of his house. As the embodiment of love, Oshun combines sexual allure and beauty with a strength that can overcome all obstacles.

Love and magic have a great deal in common. They enrich the soul, delight the heart. And they both take practice.

—**Nora Roberts,** bestselling romance author

Love is the best medicine, and there is more than enough to go around once you open your heart.

—**Julie Marie Berman,** Emmy-award-winning television actress

*He has achieved success who has lived well,
laughed often, and loved much.*

—**Bessie Stanley,** writer and poetic author of the famed
verse Success

*To fall in love is easy, even to remain in it is not
difficult; our human loneliness is cause enough.
But it is a hard quest worth making to find a
comrade through whose steady presence one
becomes steadily the person one desires to be.*

—**Anna Louise Strong,** international activist journalist

*Whatever our souls are made of, his and mine
are the same.*

—**Emily Bronte,** poet and author of the classic
Wuthering Heights

Love is a force more formidable than any other.
It is invisible–it cannot be seen or measured,
yet it is powerful enough to transform you in
a moment, and to offer you more joy than any
material possession could.

— **Barbara De Angelis,** author and
transformational teacher

Infatuation is when you think he's as sexy as Robert Redford, as smart as Henry Kissinger, as noble as Ralph Nader, as funny as Woody Allen, and as athletic as Jimmy Connors. Love is when you realize that he's as sexy as Woody Allen, as smart as Jimmy Connors, as funny as Ralph Nader, as athletic as Henry Kissinger and nothing like Robert Redford—but you'll take him anyway.

—Judith Viorst, journalist and psychoanalytic researcher

Hate leaves ugly scars; love leaves beautiful ones.

—Mignon McLaughlin, journalist and author of The Neurotic's Notebook and sequels

Love never reasons but profusely gives, like a thoughtless prodigal, it's all, and trembles lest it has done too little.

—Hannah More, poet, playwright, religious writer, and philanthropist

Love makes your soul crawl out from its hiding place.

—Zora Neale Hurston, novelist, folklorist, and anthropologist

Love is a game that two can play and both win.

—Eva Gabor, Hungarian-born actress, comedian, and singer

Badass Women Who Followed Their Bliss All the Way

Of Cockpits, Cocks and Bulls, and Other "Ladylike" Pursuits

Adalynn (Jonnie) Jonckowski: This card-carrying member of the cowgirl hall of fame has an unusual idea of a good time—hopping on the back of an angry bull and hanging on as long as possible. Called the "Belle of Billings" (Montana), she has repeatedly proved to be the world's best bull rider. Adalynn's winning attitude is evidenced here, "Any time you have the freedom to do what you want to do and exercise that freedom, you're a champ."

While Jonnie Jonckowski clings to the backs of angry Brahma bulls, Julie Krone has her own wild rides. Petite and determined, Julie Krone was the first female jockey to win the Triple Crown, a race at the Belmont Stakes. She has shown that women can ride the winning race and has $54 million worth of purses to show for it. (Jockeys keep 10 percent of the take, quite a motivator!)

Even though Julie says that "times have changed" for women, she will still occasionally be heckled with yells of "Go home, have babies, and do the dishes," when she *loses*. The wealthy winner's final comment: "In a lot of people's minds, a girl jockey is cute and delicate. With me, what you get is reckless and aggressive."

Shirley Muldowney, born Belgium Roque, took on one of the last bastions of machodom—drag racing—and came up a winner. She fell in love with cars at the age of fourteen in Schenectady, New York, racing illegally "when the police weren't looking." At fifteen, she married mechanic Jack Muldowney, and they became a hot-rodding couple. Shirley put up with enormous hostility from race fans and outright hatred from fellow drivers. In 1965, she became the first woman to operate a top-gas dragster and went on to win seventeen National Hot Rod Association titles, second only to Don Garliz. Queen of the cockpit, Shirley Muldowney became an internationally famous superstar with a critically acclaimed film about her life and achievements, *Heart Like a Wheel*.

Hockey is certainly no sport for lightweights. For many, taking shots from a bunch of big men with sticks might seem like a risky business, but to French Canadian Manon Rhéaume, it was the sport she loved. She was a goalie for the Atlanta Knights and, as such, is the first woman to have played professional hockey in the men's leagues. At five feet six and 135 pounds, Manon was slight compared to many of her team members and opponents, but she proved her ability to stop a puck. The world is finally taking note of women's ability to play this sport overall; in the year 1998, women's ice hockey became a full medal sport at the Winter Olympics, no small thanks to Manon and others like her.

Then there's Angela Hernandez, who is surely to be admired for fighting for her right to bullfight in the birthplace of machismo—Spain! In the polyester-laden year 1973, she demanded to be allowed to compete in the male-only zone of the bullring. This caused quite a commotion;

how dare she question the 1908 law forbidding women to participate in the sport of horseback bullfighting. Twenty-year-old Angela took her case all the way to the courts, where the Madrid labor court ruled in her favor, allowing her to fight, but only on foot. But threatened males found another way to thwart her—the Ministry of the Interior wouldn't issue her a license. Would-be torero Angela refused to go quietly into the Seville sunset, loudly contesting her plight, "These damned men. What do they think they are doing? Women fly planes, fight wars, and go on safaris; what's so different about fighting bulls?"

There's nothing more freeing than the shackles of love.

—**Emma Racine deFleur,** witty writer

The Eskimos had fifty-two names for snow because it was important to them: there ought to be as many for love.

—Margaret Atwood, Canadian literary critic, eco-activist, and author of The Handmaid's Tale

Nobody has ever measured, even poets, how much a heart can hold.

—Zelda Fitzgerald, novelist, painter, and socialite of the 1920s

Love, like a river, will cut a new path whenever it meets an obstacle.

—Crystal Middlemas, poetic writer

When you love someone, all your saved-up wishes start coming out.

—Elizabeth Bowen, Irish novelist and short story writer

Love is like quicksilver in the hand. Leave the fingers open and it stays. Clutch it, and it darts away.

—Dorothy Parker, deathless poet, short fiction writer, critic, and satirist of skewering wit

The truth [is] that there is only one terminal dignity—love. And the story of all love is not important—what is important is that one is capable of love. It is perhaps the only glimpse we are permitted of eternity.

—Helen Hayes, prize-winning twentieth century actress

There is only one happiness in life, to love and be loved.

—George Sand (pen name of Amantine Aurore Dupin), badass nineteenth-century French author

The best and most beautiful things in this world cannot be seen or even heard, but must be felt with the heart.

—Helen Keller, author, activist, lecturer, and the first deaf-blind person to earn a B.A.

Each time you love, love as deeply as if it were forever.

—Audre Lorde, award-winning writer, poet, and civil rights activist

The dedicated life is the life worth living. You must give with your whole heart.

—**Annie Dillard,** author of notable fiction, nonfiction, and poetry

Some people come into our lives and quickly go. Some people move our souls to dance. They awaken us to new understanding with the passing whisper of their wisdom. Some people make the sky more beautiful to gaze upon. They stay in our lives for a while, leave footprints on our hearts, and we are never the same.

—**Flavia Weedn,** prize-winning artist, illustrator, and inspirational author

> *Romance is the glamour which turns the dust of everyday life into a golden haze.*

—**Elynor Glyn,** daring English novelist and scriptwriter

> *You will manage to keep a woman in love with you only for as long as you can keep her in love with the person she becomes when she is with you.*

—**C. JoyBell C.,** inspirational author

> *I have learned not to worry about love; but to honor its coming with all my heart.*

—**Alice Walker,** award-winning author, poet, and activist

I love you—those three words have my life in them.

—Alexandra Feodorovna Romanov, last Empress of Russia, addressing her husband, Nicholas II

We can only learn to love by loving.

—Iris Murdoch, Anglo-Irish novelist and philosopher

Love is the mortar that holds the human structure together.

—Karen Casey, inspiring author

I am like a falling star who has finally found her place next to another in a lovely constellation, where we will sparkle in the heavens forever.

—**Amy Tan,** groundbreaking Chinese-American writer of The Joy Luck Club

If you have love in your life it can make up for a great many things you lack. If you don't have it, no matter what else there is, it's not enough.

—**Ann Landers,** nationally known advice columnist

Love is a choice you make from moment to moment.

—**Barbara De Angelis,** author and transformational teacher

Who so loves, believes the impossible.

—Elizabeth Barrett Browning, immortal English
Victorian poet

Love is not love if it is compelled by reason and driven by logic—love exists in spite of those things, not because of them.

—Julia Cameron, artist, poet, playwright, filmmaker, and
composer, known for The Artist's Way

That Love is all there is,
Is all we know of Love.

—Emily Dickinson, reclusive yet immortal poet

Love, Marriage, and What Comes After

We've all heard the saying; whether we like it or not, the two do seem to go together. From rhapsodizing about the lasting joys to bitching about the equally consistent irritations, women have the corner on marriage talk. The sampling below is nowhere near everything we could have said!

The married are those who have taken the terrible risk of intimacy, and having taken it, know life without intimacy to be impossible.

—Carolyn Heilbrun, feminist author and pioneering professor at Columbia

I love being married. It's so great to find that one special person you want to annoy for the rest of your life.

—**Rita Rudner,** famed stand-up comedienne

I married the first man I ever kissed. When I tell my children that, they just about throw up.

—**Barbara Bush,** devoted former First Lady

I've had an exciting time. I married for love and got a little money along with it.

—**Rose Fitzgerald Kennedy,** philanthropist and matriarch of the Kennedy clan

Marriage is a matter of give and take, but so far, I haven't been able to find anybody who'll take what I have to give.

—**Cass Daley,** singer, comedian, and actress of radio, TV, and film

Marrying a man is like buying something you've been admiring for a long time in a shop window. You may love it when you get it home, but it doesn't always go with everything else in the house.

—**Jean Kerr,** Irish-American humor writer and playwright

I must quit marrying men who feel inferior to me. Somewhere there must be a man who could be my husband and not feel inferior. I need a superior inferior man.

—Hedy Lamarr, Austrian-born actress and inventor

The trouble with some women is they get all excited about nothing—and then they marry him.

—Cher, iconic pop singer and actress

If the husband and wife can possible afford it, they should definitely have separate bathrooms for the sake of the marriage.

—Doris Day, super wholesome actress, singer, and animal welfare activist

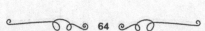

My husband and I celebrated our thirty-eighth wedding anniversary. You know what I realized? If I had killed the man the first time I thought about it, I'd have been out of jail by now.

—**Anita Miller,** funny woman

I had to really cut down on my dating.

—**Sarah Michelle Gellar,** actress and producer, on how her life changed after marriage

Before accepting a marriage proposal, take a good look at his father. If he's still handsome, witty, and has all his teeth...marry him instead.

—Diane Jordan, comedian

An archaeologist is the best husband a woman can have. The older she gets, the more interested he is in her.

—Agatha Christie, famed English mystery author

One advantage of marriage, it seems to me, is that when you fall out of love with him or he falls out of love with you, it keeps you together until maybe you fall in again.

—Judith Viorst, journalist and psychoanalytic researcher

Age does not protect you from love, but love to some extent protects you from age.

—Jeanne Moreau, French actress, singer, screenwriter, and director

No love-story has ever been told twice. I never heard any tale of lovers that did not seem to me as new as the world on its first morning.

—Eleanor Farjeon, English author of plays, poetry, biography, fiction, and satire

I truly feel that there are as many ways of loving as there are people in the world and as there are days in the life of those people.

—**Mary S. Calderone,** MD, doctor and advocate for access to birth control

But one of the attributes of love, like art, is to bring harmony and order out of chaos, to introduce meaning and affect where before there was none, to give rhythmic variations, highs and lows, to a landscape that was previously flat.

—**Molly Haskell,** feminist film/theater critic and author

Who has not found the heaven below
Will fail of it above.
God's residence is next to mine.
His furniture is love.

—**Emily Dickinson,** reclusive yet immortal poet

What the world really needs is more love and
less paperwork.

—**Pearl Bailey,** award-winning African-American actress
and singer

The person who tries to live alone will not succeed as a human being. His heart withers if it does not answer another heart. His mind shrinks away if he hears only the echoes of his own thoughts and finds no other inspiration.

—**Pearl S. Buck,** author and Nobel Prize winner

Do you want me to tell you something really subversive? Love is everything it's cracked up to be. That's why people are so cynical about it. It really is worth fighting for, being brave for, risking everything for. And the trouble is, if you don't risk anything, you risk even more.

—**Erica Jong,** controversial novelist and poet

A man has only one escape from his old self: to see a different self in the mirror of some woman's eyes.

—Clare Boothe Luce, politician and first U.S. woman in a major post as ambassador

If there is any country on earth where the course of true love may be expected to run smooth, it is America.

—Harriet Martineau, nineteenth century English social theorist and the first female sociologist

Art is not necessary at all. All that is necessary to make this world a better place to live in is to love—to love as Christ loved, as Buddha loved.

—Isadora Duncan, dancer who transformed the rules of dance

I don't want to live—I want to love first, and live incidentally.

—**Zelda Fitzgerald,** novelist, painter, and socialite of the 1920s

Love is a great beautifier.

—**Louisa May Alcott,** famed novelist and poet

Love's greatest gift is its ability to make everything it touches sacred.

—**Dr. Barbara De Angelis,** author and transformational teacher

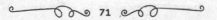

Not all of us have to possess earthshaking talent. Just common sense and love will do.

—Myrtle Auvil, author of a book on covered bridges in West Virginia

Love alone could waken love.

—Pearl S. Buck, author and Nobel Prize winner

If it is your time, love will track you down like a cruise missile.

—Lynda Barry, feminist cartoonist, author, and teacher

The All-American Girls Baseball League: Backward and in High Heels

For the briefest time in the 1940s, women had a "league of their own." And while it was not intended to be serious sports so much as a marketing package, the All-Girls Baseball League stormed the field and made it their own. The league was the brainchild of chewing gum magnate Phillip K. Wrigley, whose empire had afforded him the purchase of the Chicago Cubs. He came up with the concept of putting a bunch of sexy girls out on the field in short skirts and full makeup to entertain a baseball-starved population whose national pastime was put on hold as baseball players turned fighting men.

He was right—the gals did draw crowds, enough to field teams in several mid-sized Midwestern cities. (At the height of its popularity, the league was drawing a million paying customers per 120-game season.) A savvy businessman catering to what he believed were the tastes of baseball fans, Wrigley had strict guidelines for his "girls"—impeccable appearance and maintenance, no short hair, and no pants on or off the playing field. Pulchritude and "charm" were absolute requirements for players. Arthur Meyerhoff, chairman of the league, aptly characterized it as: "Baseball, traditionally a men's game, played by feminine type girls with masculine skill." For Meyerhoff, "feminine type" was serious business and he kept a hawk's eye on his teams for the slightest sign of lesbianism. He also sent his sandlot and cornfield trained players to charm school to keep them on their girlish toes.

Although the rules seemed stringent, the players were eager to join these new teams called the Daisies, the Lassies, the Peaches, and the Belles, because it was their only chance to play baseball professionally. Pepper Pair put it best in the book in which she and the other AAGBL (All-American Girls Professional Baseball League) players are profiled, "You have to understand that we'd rather play ball than eat, and where else could we go and get paid $100 a week to play ball?" After the war, men returned home, and major league baseball was revived. However, the All-Girls league hung on, even spawning the rival National Girl's Baseball League. With more opportunity for everyone, teams suddenly had to pay more money to their best players in order to hang on to them, and both leagues attracted players from all around the US and Canada.

Penny Marshall's wonderful film, **A League of Their Own**, did a credible job portraying the hardship and hilarity of professional women athletes trying to abide by the rules and display feminine "charm" while playing topnotch baseball. Ironically, the television boom of the fifties eroded the audience for the AAGBL as well as many other semi-pro sports. The death blow to the women's baseball leagues came, however, with the creation of the boys-only Little League. Girls no longer had a way to develop their skills in their youth and were back to sandlots and cornfields, and the AAGBL died in 1954.

The fans thought we were the best thing that ever came down the pike.

—Mary Pratt, AAGBL pitcher

Real love is a pilgrimage. It happens when there is no strategy, but it is very rare because most people are strategists.

—Anita Brookner, award-winning British art historian and novelist

Love comes when manipulation stops; when you think more about the other person than about his or her reactions to you. When you dare to reveal yourself fully. When you dare to be vulnerable.

—**Dr. Joyce Brothers,** psychologist and columnist

To love without role, without power plays, is revolution.

—**Rita Mae Brown,** pioneering lesbian author

How do I love thee? Let me count the ways. I love thee to the depth and breadth and height my soul can reach...

—**Elizabeth Barrett Browning,** immortal English Victorian poet

You can give without loving, but you cannot love without giving.

—**Amy Carmichael,** English missionary and founder of an orphanage and mission

The cure for all ills and wrongs, the cares, the sorrows, and the crimes of humanity, all lie in that one word "Love." It is the divine vitality that everywhere produces and restores life.

—**Lydia M. Child,** abolitionist writer, journalist, and activist for women's and native rights

Every day I live I am more convinced that the waste of life lies in the love we have not given, the powers we have not used, the selfish prudence that will risk nothing and which, shirking pain, misses happiness as well.

—**Mary Cholmondeley,** satiric English novelist

Love makes the wildest spirit tame, and the tamest spirit wild.

—**Alexis Delp,** author and bohemienne

I know that I can give love for a minute, for half an hour, for a day, for a month, but I can give, and I'm very happy to do that and I want to do that.

—**Diana,** Princess of Wales

I argue thee that love is life. And life hath immortality.

—Emily Dickinson, reclusive yet immortal poet

We've grown to be one soul-two parts; our lives so intertwined that when some passion stirs your heart, I feel the quake in mine.

—Gloria Gaither, gospel songwriter, author, and speaker

Love have nothing to do with what you are expecting to get, only what you are expecting to give-which is everything.

—Katherine Hepburn, classic Hollywood leading lady

> *Love is a force that connects us to every strand of the universe, an unconditional state that characterizes human nature, a form of knowledge that is always there for us if only we can open ourselves to it.*

—Emily H. Sell, author and editor of a book on love

Falling in love consists merely in uncorking the imagination and bottling the common sense.

—Helen Rowland, columnist and humorist

To infinite, ever present Love, all is Love, and there is no error, no sin, sickness, nor death.

—**Mary Baker Eddy,** founder of the Church of Christ, Scientist

Put love first. Entertain thoughts that give life. And when a thought or resentment, or hurt, or fear comes your way, have another thought that is more powerful–a thought that is love.

—**Mary Manin Morrissey,** motivational speaker

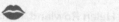

You never lose by loving. You always lose by holding back.

—**Barbara DeAngelis,** author and transformational teacher

Sleeping alone, except under doctor's orders, does much harm. Children will tell you how lonely it is sleeping alone. If possible, you should always sleep with someone you love. You both recharge your mutual batteries free of charge.

—**Marlene Dietrich,** German singer and actress of distinction

When someone loves you, the way they say your name is different. You know your name is safe in their mouth.

—**Jess C Scott,** artist, entrepreneur, and author with an edge from Singapore, in *The Intern*

There isn't any formula or method. You learn to love by loving—by paying attention and doing what one thereby discovers has to be done.

—Helen Hayes, prize-winning twentieth century actress

To love is to receive a glimpse of heaven.

—Karen Sunde, award-winning screenwriter
and playwright

*There is always something left to love.
And if you haven't learned that, you ain't
learned nothing.*

—Lorraine Hansberry, renowned African-American
playwright and writer

Love involves a peculiar unfathomable combination of understanding and misunderstanding.

—Diane Arbus, distinguished photographer who focused on the marginalized

It is better to break one's heart than to do nothing with it.

—Margaret Kennedy, English playwright and novelist

Love is always present; it is just a matter of feeling it or not.

—Kimberly Kirberg, inspiring author

To love means not to impose your own powers on your fellow man but to offer him your help. And if he refuses it, to be proud that he can do it on his own strength.

—**Elizabeth Kubler-Ross,** pioneering Swiss-American psychiatrist and writer

Love is the emblem of eternity; it confounds all notions of time; effaces all memory of beginning, all fear of an end.

—**Madame de Staël,** eighteenth-century woman of letters

Life is infested with ordinariness, and there is no reason why love should be, too.

—**Daphne Rose Kingma,** bestselling author and speaker on love and relationships

The more connections you and your lover make, not just between your bodies, but between your minds, your hearts, and your souls, the more you will strengthen the fabric of your relationship, and the more real moments you will experience together.

—**Barbara De Angelis,** author and transformational teacher

One kind word can warm three winter months.

—**Mary Jane Ryan,** bestselling author and executive coach

To love deeply in one direction makes us more loving in all others.

—**Madame Anne Swetchine,** Russian mystic and Parisian salonist

Love means never having to say "What?"

—**Autumn Stephens,** author of the Wild Women series, editor, and essayist

What did my hands do before they held you?

—**Sylvia Plath,** renowned poet and fiction writer

CHAPTER 2

Love, Lust, and What We Wore

You won't find two things that rule the world more than lust or love. Whether it's a lust for power or a hunger for a romantic love, these emotions find their places in everyone's thoughts. And women are no exemption. Just like anyone, we wrestle with the same feelings, pining after that hot guy at the bar the other night, or the friend who is turning into more than a friend. There's a thin line between love and lust, and we all try to find it with our significant others while also balancing everything else in our lives.

But whether you are reclusive or entirely open about your experiences with love and lust, it's hard to deny the frustration that can come from experiencing these emotions. We've all had to endure the "oh, it's that time of the month" comments, or the dreadful "let's talk about us" comments. All because for some reason we feel the need to be loved, or get caught up in lustful longings.

Well, these women have felt the same frustration, experienced the same difficulties in their own love lives, and lived to tell the story. Read on for quotes that will make you appreciate your own love all the more, and to find someone who put into words exactly how you feel about that one you can't get over.

Lovers are like roses—best by the dozen.

—**Barbara La Marr,** 1920s film actress and screenwriter

You know more about a guy in one night in bed than you do in months of conversation. In the sack, they can't cheat.

—**Edith Piaf,** legendary French cabaret singer, songwriter, and actress

It's never easy keeping your own husband happy. It's much easier to make someone else's husband happy.

—**Zsa Zsa Gabor,** Hungarian-American actress and socialite

I love the lines men use to get us into bed. "Please, I'll only put it in for a minute." What am I, a microwave?

—**Beverly Mickins,** TV personality and actress

If someone had told me years ago that sharing a sense of humor was so vital to partnerships, I could have avoided a lot of sex!

—**Kate Beckinsale,** brilliant English actress

Badass Amelia Bloomer: Free Your *** and Your Mind Will Follow

"Drag" had a whole different meaning for nineteenth century fashion plates! Women were wearing fifteen pounds worth of skirts and petticoats until the 1850s, when Amelia Bloomer started advocating wearing a radical new undergarment in her new circular, *The Lily*, the first journal by and for women. Amelia was inspired to try this liberating new costume when she was visited by Elizabeth Cady Stanton and her cousin, Elizabeth Miller. While abroad, Miller was motivated to unburden herself of several pounds of skirts and created a Turkish-inspired short skirt and pantaloon combo that offered much comfort and freedom of movement. Stanton and Bloomer jumped into pairs of drawers with both feet, and Bloomer sang the praises of their new couture option in her magazine, "Fit yourselves for a higher sphere and cease groveling in the dirt. Let there be no stain of earth upon your soul or apparel." The pantaloons proved to be an overnight sensation with scores of women sending in requests for patterns. The regular press lampooned the 'loons as "Bloomerism" and thus were born "bloomers."

> *Among men, sex sometimes results in intimacy; among women, intimacy sometimes results in sex.*

—Dame Barbara Cartland, bestselling English romance writer

> *A homely face and no figure have aided women heavenward.*

—Minna Antrim, author known for her turn-of-the-century collection of toasts

> *If God had wanted women to be sex symbols, he wouldn't have made Mary a virgin.*

—Patti Harrison and Robin Tyler, pioneering lesbian feminist comedy duo

However much men say sex is not on their mind all the time, it is most of the time.

—**Jackie Collins,** English romance novelist
and screenwriter

Lovers should also have their days off.

—**Natalie Clifford Barney,** American expatriate
playwright, poet, novelist, and Parisian salonist

Any woman who thinks the way to a man's heart is through his stomach is aiming about ten inches too high.

—**Adrienne Gusoff,** humorist, freelance writer, and
advice columnist

I have more sex appeal on the tip of my nose than many women in their entire bodies.

—**Audrey Hepburn,** piquant actress, dancer, and humanitarian

I was like, "I want that one!"

—**Jessica Simpson,** pop singer and actress, on her initial attraction to Nick Lachey

I am not especially defined by my sex life, nor complete without it.

—**Paula Gunn Allen,** Native American lesbian poet, professor, literary critic, and activist

Personally, I like sex, and I don't care what a man thinks of me as long as I get what I want from him—which is usually sex.

—Valerie Perrine, film actress, Vegas showgirl, and public nudity pioneer

If men knew what women laughed about, they would never sleep with us.

—Erica Jong, controversial novelist and poet

Everybody should practice safe sex. 'Cause nobody wants to be doing it and put an eye out.

—Emmy Gay, feminist "Fusion Art" comedian

Women complain about sex more than men. Their gripes fall into two major categories: (1) Not enough. (2) Too much.

—**Ann Landers,** nationally known advice columnist

For women the best aphrodisiacs are words. The G-spot is in the ears. He who looks for it below there is wasting his time.

—**Isabel Allende,** noted Chilean-American "magic realism" author

Some men know that a light touch of the tongue, running from a woman's toes to her ears, lingering in the softest way possible in between, given often enough and sincerely enough, would add immeasurably to world peace.

—Marianne Williamson, spiritual teacher and author

No one ever expects a great lay to pay all the bills.

—Jean Harlow, leading lady of 1930s film

Sex: That pathetic shortcut suggested by nature, the supreme joker, as a remedy for our loneliness, that ephemeral communion which we persuade ourselves to be of the spirit when in fact it is only of the body—durable not even in memory!

—**Vita Sackville-West,** English poet, novelist, and journalist

Dr. Ruth says we should tell our lovers how to make love to us. My boyfriend goes nuts if I tell him how to drive!

—**Pam Stone,** actress, comedian, writer, and talk show host

Ah, the sex thing. I'm glad that part of my life is over.

—Greta Garbo, sultry Swedish-born actress of the 1920s–1930s, at sixty-nine

Size Actually Matters

When it comes to conversations about sex, there's one topic that almost always comes up eventually. Although women can never agree on it, the matter of size certainly plays a role in our sex lives—or at least our sex gossip.

According to darling Merle Oberon, Jimmy Cagney was "a REALLY big star!"

If Clark had one inch less, he'd be the "queen of Hollywood" instead of "the king."

—**Carole Lombard,** 1930s film actress and Clark Gable's third wife

He's no Tommy Lee, that's for sure.

—**Unimpressed publicist,** upon seeing paparazzi pics of Jude Law caught naked on camera

In the United States of America, there are over 25,000 sex phone lines for men. You know how many there are for women? Just three. Apparently for women, if we want someone to talk dirty and nasty to us, we'll just go to work.

—**Felicia Michaels,** provocative stand-up comedian

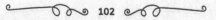

I need sex for a clear complexion, but I'd rather do it for love.

—**Joan Crawford,** classic grande dame actress of film and television

I haven't had sex in eight months. To be honest, I now prefer bowling.

—**Lil' Kim,** provocative rapper, record producer, and actress

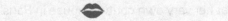

If sex is such a natural phenomenon, how come there are so many books on how to do it?

—**Bette Midler,** inimitable actress, singer/songwriter, film producer, and comedian

Badass Fashionista Gabrielle "Coco" Chanel: "A woman should be two things—classy and fabulous!"

Considered by many to be the mother of modern fashion, Gabrielle "Coco" Chanel was the first fashion designer to create clothes that matched emerging attitudes of women on greater freedom and independence. Born in France around 1883, Coco's first step toward a life in the fashion industry was a job at a hatmaker's shop in Deauville, France, where she worked until 1912. At thirty-one years old, she struck out on her own and opened her very own shop featuring streamlined and unfussy wool jersey dresses. Her strikingly new yet simple style caught on quickly. Chanel's success with the dresses and the celebratory atmosphere following World War I encouraged her to really go to town with smartly cut suits, sophisticated short skirts, and bold, chunky jewelry designed at her very own couture house in Paris!

In 1922, she created Chanel No. 5, the perfume every woman wanted, named for her lucky number; to this day, it remains one of the all-time favorite perfumes. Chanel's innovations are legendary—costume jewelry, evening scarves, short skirts, and the little black dress all came from the steel-trap mind of Coco Chanel. She retired in 1938, but got bored and staged a remarkably successful comeback in the mid-fifties.

Coco, the ultimate Frenchwoman, never married, but seemed to be utterly happy with her career as an independent businesswoman in charge of her own time and her own life. She made America's Horatio Alger look shabby—the daughter of a vagabond street peddler, she was raised in orphanages and went on to found an empire, live a busy glamorous life, and leave behind a legacy that will last forever. The idol of practically everyone in the industry, Coco Chanel was the epitome of the modern woman. Yves St. Laurent once called her "the Godmother of us all," and French surrealist Jean Cocteau remarked, "(Coco Chanel) has, by a kind of miracle, worked in fashion according to

rules that would seem to have value for painters,
musicians, poets."

There have been many Duchesses of Westminster, but there is only one Coco Chanel.

—designer **Coco Chanel** on why she dropped a
prominent wooer

It is not sex that gives the pleasure, but the lover.

—**Marge Piercy,** quintessential poet, novelist,
and activist

It doesn't make any difference what you do in the bedroom as long as you don't do it in the street and frighten the horses.

—Mrs. Patrick Campbell, English Victorian actress

I think the V line below a man's stomach is just really beautiful and sexy.

—Kirstie Allie, actress and comedian

The argument between wives and whores is an old one; each one thinking that whatever she is, at least she is not the other.

—Andrea Dworkin, radical feminist author and anti-porn activist

I smoked a lot of dope. I made it with a lot of guys. I tried everything I could think of to act as bad and outrageous as I could.

—**Elizabeth Ashley,** Tony Award-winning actress of stage and screen

So, this is where I get laid!

—silent film actress **Olive Thomas** on her initial meeting with film exec. David O. Selznick at his casting couch-equipped office

I like to drink and f**k.

—**Louise Brooks,** iconic flapper actress of the silver screen

Sexual love is the most stupendous facet of the universe, and the most magical mystery our poor blind senses know.

—**Amy Lowell,** leading Imagist poet and Pulitzer Prize winner

I've learned one hell of a lot about men in my lifetime. They're all right to take to bed, but you sure better never let them get a stranglehold on you.

—**Blaze Starr,** inventive stripper and burlesque star

Men are my hobby; if I ever got married, I'd have to give it up.

—**Mae West,** memorable actress, comedian, screenwriter, and sex symbol

CHAPTER 3

Love Hurts (Sometimes)

You can blame the media, you can point the finger at your peers, you can find fault in your upbringing; you can fault whoever you want, but you can't deny that little voice constantly telling you that you need to be beautiful, even perfect. So, answering this little voice, we pluck, we diet, we wax, we cover up, and we try to reach physical perfection. But why? It seems to be mostly because someone or something told us that, most importantly, we need to be pretty on the outside.

But as life teaches us year after year, it isn't the pedicures, the highlights, or the Spanx that make us beautiful, it's confidence. If you feel your best wearing lipstick and mascara, rock it, you look beautiful. If you prefer patchouli to perfume, own that aroma and be your best self. You see, the secret to being beautiful lies in knowing you always are. After all, confidence is the best accessory a girl can have.

In this chapter, you will find quotes from badass women who know that they are beautiful, no matter what society, peers, or parents say. From world-class lovelies to lipstick lesbians to the-hell-with-it ex-hippies, not one of the ladies quoted herein wants to quell your quest to look cute. Nor, for that matter, will you be counseled to schedule a Brazilian. There is a distinct possibility in this next chapter, however, that you will find yourself inspired to work on your inner self with the same fervor that you devote to your exterior.

I know who I am. I am not perfect. I am not the most beautiful woman in the world. But I'm one of them.

—**Mary J. Blige,** R & B and hip hop/soul singer, songwriter, and producer

The beauty of a woman is not in a facial mode, but the true beauty in a woman is reflected in her soul. It is the caring that she lovingly gives, the passion that she shows. The beauty of a woman grows with the passing years.

—**Audrey Hepburn,** piquant actress, dancer, and humanitarian

No matter what a woman looks like, if she's confident, she's sexy.

—Paris Hilton, heiress, media celebrity, and businesswoman

Being jealous of a beautiful woman is not going to make you more beautiful.

—Zsa Zsa Gabor, Hungarian-American actress and socialite

I blame my mother for my poor sex life. All she told me was, "The man goes on top and the woman underneath." For three years my husband and I slept in bunk beds.

—Joan Rivers, acerbic queen of comedy

It's not vanity to feel you have a right to be beautiful. Women are taught to feel we're not good enough, that we must live up to someone else's standards. But my aim is to cherish myself as I am.

—**Elle Macpherson,** supermodel, actress, and
TV personality

Taking joy in living is a woman's best cosmetic.

—**Rosalind Russell,** actress, comedian, and singer

I'm not a stereotypically beautiful woman, and I'm so happy that I'm not. I've seen those ladies—the need to be attractive at all times is ghastly. Also, in your twenties, if you are beautiful, everything comes to you, so you never need to develop a personality. I never had that problem.

—**Miranda Hart,** English comedian and actress

I always thought that people told you that you're beautiful—that this was a title that was bestowed upon you.... I think that it's time to take this power into our own hands and to say, "You know what? I'm beautiful. I just am. And that's my light. I'm just a beautiful woman."

—**Margaret Cho,** renowned stand-up comedian, actress, designer, and author

I love men, even though they're lying, cheating scumbags.

—Gwyneth Paltrow, starring actress, singer, and food writer

If a man lies to you, don't get mad, get even. I once dated a guy who waited three months into our relationship before he told me he was married. I said, "Hey, don't worry about it. I used to be a man."

—Livia Squires, doubly brainy seismologist and incisive comedienne

I'm single. I'm skinny. I still can't find a man.

—**Sarah Ferguson,** Duchess of York, writer and
film producer

*If love means never having to say you're sorry,
then marriage means always having to say
everything twice.*

—**Estelle Getty,** comedian and actress known for The
Golden Girls

*My biggest problem with dating is that I have no
game. Some women can just bat their eyes and
men come running. The men just keep popping
up one after another. It's like they have a
magical man-filled Pez dispenser.*

—**Lori Giarnella,** comedian by night, digital media
manager by day

The essence of romantic love is that wonderful beginning, after which sadness and impossibility may become the rule.

—Anita Brookner, award-winning English art historian and novelist

We choose those we like; with those we love, we have no say in the matter.

—Mignon McLaughlin, journalist and author of The Neurotic's Notebook and sequels

If it has tires or testicles, you're going to have trouble with it.

—bumper sticker

Saying that men talk about basketball in order to avoid talking about their feelings is the same as saying that women talk about their feelings in order to avoid talking about baseball.

—**Deborah Tannen,** linguistics professor and author on communicating

Women might be able to fake orgasms. But men can fake whole relationships.

—**Sharon Stone,** award-winning actress and film producer

With lovers like men, who needs torturers?

—**Susanne Kappeler,** professor and freelance writer

I'm like the Statue of Liberty. No one wants to pay for the upkeep, but everybody wants to say they've been there.

—**Priscilla Davis,** wealthy Texan divorcée socialite and survivor

Opposites attract—and then aggravate.

—**Joy Browne,** clinical psychologist with an advice counselor radio show

Falling in love is absolutely no way of getting to know someone.

—**Sheila Sullivan,** twentieth century psychologist

The advantage of love at first sight is that it delays a second sight.

—Natalie Clifford Barney, American expatriate playwright, poet, novelist, and Parisian salonist

For me, on a scale of one to ten, romance comes about eight, after chess but before politics and football.

—Alice Thomas Ellis, British essayist, novelist, and cookbook writer

All love shifts and changes. I don't know if you can be wholeheartedly in love all the time.

—Dame Julie Andrews, actress, singer, and children's author

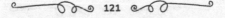

Giving a man space is like giving a dog a computer: the chances are he will not use it wisely.

—Bette-Jane Raphael, journalist and essayist

Sometimes I wonder if men and women really suit each other; perhaps they should live next door and just visit now and then.

—Katharine Hepburn, classic Hollywood leading lady

The pain of love is the pain of being alive. It is perpetual wound.

—Maureen Duffy, English writer, poet, playwright, and gay rights/animal rights activist

The easiest kind of relationship for me is with ten thousand people. The hardest is with one.

—Joan Baez, folk singer, songwriter, musician, and activist

It is better to be unfaithful without wanting to be.

—Brigitte Bardot, sultry actress, singer, dancer, and later animal rights activist

We Women Love Movies About Love

Painful love often makes for some unpainful storylines. Here's a list of the weepiest chick flicks ever—grab a box of Kleenex, some chocolate, your best girlfriends, and turn the channel to "romance!"

The Way We Were

Featuring Barbra Streisand and Robert Redford as star-crossed soulmates— "Gorgeous goy guy" meets radical Jewish girl in this glossy romance.

Camille

Scandinavian siren Greta Garbo stars as a tragic courtesan turned heroine who has to sacrifice her own happiness in order to prove her love; a classic for all time.

The French Lieutenant's Woman

A movie from a book about a movie about a movie. Confused? Don't worry, just sit back and enjoy Meryl Streep at her most mesmerizing in her role as a woman abandoned by her French lieutenant lover, played by the stellar Jeremy Irons.

The Woman

Starring Rosalind Russell, Norma Shearer, and Joan Crawford, the movie's tagline says it all: "The stars! The clothes! The cruelty! The catfights!" Husband-stealing vixens at each other's throats is also a fairly good description.

The English Patient

Mysterious count Ralph Fiennes has an affair with lovely Englishwoman Kristen Scott Thomas. This romance takes you to northern Africa and Italy during World War II. Passion, danger, spies, lies, and redemption...what could be better?

Bull Durham

A romantic comedy love triangle featuring a majorly minor league baseball team, an aging groupie, a world-weary catcher, and a cocky rookie. Kevin Costner, Susan Sarandon, and Tim Robbins heat up on the screen and in real life, too!

The hardest-learned lesson: that people have only their kind of love to give, not our kind.

—**Mignon McLaughlin,** journalist and author of The Neurotic's Notebook and sequels

Part of the reason that men seem so much less loving than women is that men's behavior is measured with a feminine ruler.

—**Francesca M.** Cancian, sociology professor

Love is an exploding cigar we willingly smoke.

—**Lynda Barry,** feminist cartoonist, author, and teacher

We don't believe in rheumatism and true love until after the first attack.

—**Baroness Marie** von Ebner-Eschenbach, Austrian author noted for psychological novels

Romance is dead—it was acquired in a hostile takeover by Hallmark and Disney, homogenized, and sold off piece by piece.

—**Lisa Simpson,** superpowered nerd girl cartoon character on *The Simpsons*

Mumps, measles, and puppy love are terrible after twenty.

—**Mignon McLaughlin,** journalist and author of *The Neurotic's Notebook* and sequels

Before I met my husband, I'd never fallen in love. I'd stepped in it a few times.

—**Rita Rudner,** famed stand-up comedienne

Love, love, love—all the wretched cant of it, masking egotism, lust, masochism, fantasy under a mythology of sentimental postures.

—**Germaine Greer,** untamed feminist professor, author, and intellectual

Life is a quest and love a quarrel.

—**Edna St. Vincent Millay,** renowned poet and playwright

Have you ever been in love? Horrible, isn't it? It makes you so vulnerable. It opens your chest and it opens your heart, and it means someone can get inside you and mess you up. You build up all these defenses. You build up this whole armor for years so nothing can hurt you, then one stupid person, no different from any other stupid person, wanders into your stupid life...

—**Rose Walker,** graphic novel heroine of Neil Gaiman's Sandman series

There are men I could spend eternity with, but not this life.

—**Kathleen Norris,** bestselling poet and essayist

If only one could tell true love from false love as one can tell mushrooms from toadstools.

—**Katherine Mansfield,** New Zealand-born modernist short story writer

It was the men I deceived the most that I loved the most.

—**Marguerite Duras,** French writer, playwright, and experimental film director

Romantic love, in pornography as in life, is the mythic celebration of female negation. For a woman, love is defined as her willingness to submit to her own annihilation. The proof of love is that she is willing to be destroyed by the one whom she loves, for his sake.

—**Andrea Dworkin,** radical feminist author and anti-porn activist

Well, love is insanity. The ancient Greeks knew that. It is the taking over of a rational and lucid mind by delusion and self-destruction. You lose yourself, you have no power over yourself, you can't even think straight.

—**Marilyn French,** bestselling radical feminist author

In a great romance, each person plays a part the other really likes.

—Elizabeth Ashley, Tony Award-winning actress of stage and screen

The fate of love is that it always seems too little or too much.

—Amelia Barr, British novelist and teacher

Love ceases to be a pleasure when it ceases to be a secret.

—Aphra Behn, Seventeenth century playwright, poet, translator, and novelist

Love matches are made by people who are content, for a month of honey, to condemn themselves to a life of vinegar.

—**Marguerite Gardiner,** Irish nineteenth century journalist, novelist, and literary hostess

Love is not enough. It must be the foundation, the cornerstone—but not the complete structure. It is much too pliable, too yielding.

—**Bette Davis,** magnetic actress of stage and screen

Badass FLOTUS (First Lady of the United States) Eleanor Roosevelt: She Always Did the Thing She Could Not Do (Admirably So, Too)

Eleanor was born Anne Eleanor Roosevelt and came from colonial stock on both sides of her family. Though born to the privileged class, she reached out to all women, regardless of economic status, and they responded, knowing she was a kindred soul. She preferred to do good works at settlement houses among the working class rather than party at snooty salons. Eleanor also snuck in an engagement to her fifth cousin, political aspirant Franklin Delano Roosevelt. They quickly had six children, and the burgeoning clan found themselves in the District of Columbia while FDR served as assistant secretary of the navy. It was there that Eleanor discovered his affair with Lucy Mercer, her social secretary. She was devastated, but found an inner resolve to withstand the pain and became even more dedicated to social change.

When FDR was elected president, Eleanor was less than thrilled with her status as First Lady. But she took on the job and made it her own. She held a press conference in 1933, a first for a First Lady, and regularly spoke with a corps of women reporters. While FDR had his first fireside chats, Eleanor had "My Day," a newspaper column and radio show that she used as pulpit to address many social justice issues. After her husband's death, she continued with her work, becoming a delegate to the United Nations and helping launch UNICEF. This strong humanitarian woman is still one of the most cherished figures in history.

One would always want to think of oneself as being on the side of love, ready to recognize it and wish it well—but, when confronted with it in others, one so often resented it, questioned its true nature, secretly dismissed the particular instance as folly or promiscuity. Was it merely jealousy, or a reluctance to admit so noble and enviable a sentiment in anyone but oneself?

—**Shirley Hazzard,** Australian-born fiction writer and essayist

Women are like dogs really. They love like dogs, a little insistently. And they like to fetch and carry and come back wistfully after hard words, and learn rather quickly to carry a basket.

—**Mary Roberts Rinehart,** mystery writer often called "the American Agatha Christie"

Smart women love smart men more than smart men love smart women.

—Natalie Portman, Israeli-American actress and Harvard grad

I have never wanted to be one of those girls in love with boys who would not have me. Unrequited love–plain desperate aboveboard boy-chasing–turned you into a salesperson, and what you were selling was something he didn't want, could not use, would never miss. Unrequited love was deciding to be useless, and I could never abide uselessness.

—Elizabeth McCracken, fiction writer and creative writing professor

I have yet to hear a man ask for advice on how to combine marriage and a career.

—Gloria Steinem, journalist, activist, and feminist founder of Ms. Magazine

Great passions, my dear, don't exist: they're liars' fantasies. What do exist are little loves that may last for a short or a longer while.

—Anna Magnani, tempestuous actress

We live in a terrible world. A man kisses your hand, and it's screamed out from all the headlines. He can't even tell you he loves you without the whole world knowing about it.

—Grace Kelly, actress who became princess of Monaco by marriage

Marriage—it is like signing your life away.

—**Julie Christie,** legendary British actress and icon of
London in the '60s

He's the equivalent of a dirt sandwich.

—**Sharon Stone,** award-winning actress and film
producer, describing her ex

He thought more of making love to the camera than to me.

—silent film actress **Jean Acker**, who divorced Rudolph
Valentino after a six-hour marriage

Lovers are at all times insufferable; but when the holy laws of matrimony give them the right to be so amazingly fond and affectionate, it makes one sick.

—**Lady Caroline Lamb,** Anglo-Irish aristocrat and novelist most renowned for her affair with Lord Byron

💋

Don't settle for a relationship that won't let you be yourself.

—**Oprah Winfrey,** media entrepreneur, producer, talk show host, and self-made philanthropist

💋

CHAPTER 4

Womanly Wisdom: Love Lost and Found

From day one, gender shapes your experience of the world and how the world experiences you. In the big picture, maybe the distinction between male and female is irrelevant. But in our daily lives, nothing is more crucial than whether we queue up outside the ladies' room or stride straight into the (strangely vacant!) men's.

Just imagine how it would feel—and how much time it would save—if you could just jump out of bed in the morning, do nothing more than run a comb through your hair, and consider yourself presentable. To meet someone new and not have to worry about potential child-rearing as a consequence. (Now that's a *real* timesaver for you.) Or to walk home alone at night without your keys between your fingers.

In other words, there's a good reason that we sometimes feel that we have more in common with some random woman just ahead of us in the grocery store line than we do with our own boyfriends and husbands. We do.

The issues addressed in this final chapter vary wildly from instructions on how you should cry to addressing the particular challenges of dinner parties. The common experience of womanhood—with all its profound plusses, with all its maddening minuses—abounds in each commentator's remarks. Listen, and you'll hear incitement to rebel against sexism. You'll hear the cry for reform of every stripe. These are the quotes from badass women that you never knew you needed.

A wise woman wishes to be no one's enemy; a wise woman refuses to be anyone's victim.

—**Maya Angelou,** distinguished poet, memoirist, and civil rights activist

I declare to you that woman must not depend upon the protection of man, but must be taught to protect herself, and there I take my stand.

—**Susan B. Anthony,** women's rights activist and social reformer

I am grateful to be a woman. I must have done something great in another life.

—Maya Angelou, distinguished poet, memoirist, and civil rights activist

One of the best things that happened to me is that I'm a woman. That is the way all females should feel.

—Marilyn Monroe, iconic actress and singer

The state controlling a woman would mean denying her full autonomy and full equality.

—Ruth Bader Ginsburg, Supreme Court Justice

I never realized until lately that women were supposed to be the inferior sex.

—Katharine Hepburn, classic Hollywood leading lady

Never give up, for that is just the place and time that the tide will turn.

—Harriet Beecher Stowe, abolitionist, author, and editor

When two people decide to get a divorce, it isn't a sign that they "don't understand" one another, but a sign that they have, at last, begun to.

—Helen Rowland, columnist and humorist

I've had diseases that lasted longer than my marriages.

—Nell Carter, singer and actress of stage and screen

Love lasts about seven years. That's how long it takes for the cells of the body to totally replace themselves.

—Francoise Sagan, French playwright, novelist, and screenwriter

It's afterward you realize that the feeling of happiness you had with a man didn't necessarily prove that you loved him.

—Marguerite Duras, French writer, playwright, and experimental film director

We were incompatible in a lot of ways. Like, for example, I was a night person, and he didn't like me.

—Wendy Liebman, comic with mastery of subtle stand-up style

My attitude toward men who mess around is simple: if you find 'em, kill 'em.

—Loretta Lynn, country classic singer-songwriter

Love never dies of starvation, but often of indigestion.

—Ninon de l'Enclos, Seventeenth century French author, freethinker, courtesan, and patron of the arts

Badass Isadora Duncan:
Her Life Was a Dance

Isadora née Angela Duncan was born in San Francisco on a summer's day in 1877. Brought up in the manner of fallen aristocracy by her poor mother, a music teacher, young Angela studied classical ballet, but soon discarded the rules in favor of her own freer, interpretive dance. Her public debut of this new style of dance was a total flop in New York City and Chicago, so she scraped together some savings and headed for Europe on board a cattle boat.

In London, she studied the sculptures of pagan Greece and integrated the sense of movement from these classical remnants into her dance practice. A grande dame of the British stage, Mrs. Patrick Campbell, became the young American's patron and set up private dance salons for Isadora at the homes of the most cultured crème de la crème. Soon, snooty Brits couldn't get enough of the barefoot and beautiful young nymph, dancing her heart out in a dryad costume that left very little guesswork as to Duncan's anatomy. Soon she was packing theaters and concert halls all over the continent. In 1905, she toured Russia as well.

Isadora Duncan was not only the dance diva of her day, but a woman who dared to flout social convention, bearing children out of wedlock (wedlock was a notion utterly repugnant to Duncan and her pack) to stage designer Gordon Craig as well as Paris Singer of the sewing machine dynasty. But her life was not all roses—Duncan lost her two babies and their nurse when their car rolled into the Seine and all three drowned. Duncan tried to sublimate her grief in work, opening dance schools around Europe and touring South America, Germany, and France.

In 1920, she received an invitation to establish a school in the Soviet Union, where she fell in undying love with Sergey Aleksandrovich Yesenin, a respected poet half her age. The two married despite Duncan's abhorrence of the institution, and were taken for Bolshevik spies as they traveled the globe. Upon being heckled mercilessly at a performance in Boston's Symphony Hall, Isadora Duncan bid her homeland adieu forever: "Goodbye America, I shall never see you again!" She was as good as her word; the honeymooners scuttled back to Europe, where their relationship crashed against the rocks of Yesenin's insanity. He committed suicide in 1925, and Duncan lived the remainder of her life on the French Riviera, where another auto accident ended her life. One of her dramatic Greek-inspired scarves got tangled in the wheel of her car, and she was strangled.

Though her life was wild and messy, Isadora Duncan's real triumph was her art. She changed the dance world forever, freeing the form from Victorian constriction to allow more natural movement. Duncan believed in celebrating the sculptural beauty of the female body and that dance, at its zenith, was "divine expression." Duncan is regarded by many to have been the chief pioneer of modern dance. She was a free spirit who believed that "to dance is to live."

If my art is symbolic of any one thing, it is symbolic of the freedom of woman and her emancipation.

—**Isadora Duncan,** dancer who transformed the rules of dance

There were three of us in the marriage, so it was a bit crowded.

—**Diana,** Princess of Wales

I still miss my ex-husband, but my aim is improving.

—Seen on a sign

I have always found husbands much more satisfying after marriage than during.

—**Peggy Guggenheim,** philanthropic art collector, bohemian, and socialite

Don't put an absurdly high value on him. Think of the millions of other girls doing without him, yet able to bear it!

—**Orfea Sybil,** bohemienne of bon mots

I'm not upset about my divorce; I am only upset I'm not a widow.

—Unknown wild woman

I should be groaning over the sins I have committed, but I can only sigh for what I have lost.

—Héloïse, medieval French nun, writer, scholar, and romantic correspondent of the famed scholar Abelard

I still miss those I loved who are no longer with me, but I find I am grateful for having loved them. The gratitude has finally conquered the loss.

—Rita Mae Brown, pioneering lesbian author

Brilliant Badass Simone de Beauvoir: Individuality and Intellect

Existentialist writer Simone de Beauvoir was the leader of the feminist movement in France. Her book, *The Second Sex*, immediately took a place of importance in the feminist canon upon its publication in 1949 and established Beauvoir's reputation as a first-rate thinker. Although her brutally honest examination of the condition of women in the first half of the twentieth century shocked some delicate sensibilities, others were gratified to have someone tell it like it was. Beauvoir described the traditional female roles of wife and mother as that of "relative beings" dependent on context. She urged women to go after careers and endeavor to achieve fulfillment through meaningful work.

Beauvoir avoided the trap of "relative being" (and nothingness) by remaining partners and lovers with Jean-Paul Sartre, whom she met in her early twenties in a salon study group at

Paris' famed university, the Sorbonne. They recognized each other as soulmates immediately and stayed together for fifty-one years in a highly unorthodox partnership wherein they left openings for "contingent loves" so as not to limit their capacity for enriching experience. She eschewed motherhood and all forms of domesticity; the duo rarely dined at home, preferring cafes for all their meals. They lived together only very briefly during World War II and had difficulty protecting their privacy as word of the trendy new existentialist philosophy, ultimately espousing ambiguity, spread and their international prestige heightened. While Sartre is generally credited as the creator of existentialism, Simone was no philosophical slouch. Her treatise *Existentialism and the Wisdom of the Ages* postulates the human condition as neutral, neither inherently good nor evil, "[The individual] is nothing at first," she theorized, "It is up to him to make himself good or bad depending upon whether he assumes his freedom or denies it."

Beauvoir's first efforts toward a writing career were fictional, including her aptly titled maiden voyage as a novelist in 1943's *She Came to Stay*, a fictionalization of Sartre's youthful protégée Olga Kosakiewicz, who entered into a triangular living relationship with the two French intellectuals. Next, she tackled the male point of view in her epic novel examining death in *All Men Are Mortal*, whose central character was an immortal her novel tracked for seven centuries. In 1954, after the success of her feminist classic *The Second Sex*, Beauvoir returned to fiction with *The Mandarins*, a novelization of the splintered and disenchanted French intelligentsia, which won the illustrious Goncourt Prize.

She continued to write and publish, creating a weighty body of work. She outlived Sartre and died on a Parisian summer day in 1986 after a long and thoughtful life, leaving a legacy of significant contributions to gender and identity issues as well as philosophy and literature.

One is not born, but rather becomes, a woman.

—**Simone de Beauvoir,** intellectual, writer, philosopher, and social theorist (Opening line of The Second Sex)

In Hollywood, an equitable divorce settlement means each party getting fifty percent of the publicity.

—**Lauren Bacall,** siren singer and iconic actress

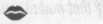

To live in this world, you must be able to do three things: to love what is mortal; to hold it against your bones, knowing your own life depends on it; and, when the time comes to let it go, to let it go.

—**Mary Oliver,** Pulitzer Prize-winning nature poet

> **Moments of kindness and reconciliation are worth having, even if the parting has to come sooner or later.**
>
> —**Alice Munro,** groundbreaking short story writer and Nobel Prize winner

> **Have some good revenge fantasies. Hate his guts if that makes you feel better!**
>
> —**Marni Kamins,** Breakup Repair and Dating Repair author and therapist

> **Deep down, we knew there wasn't a forever plan.**
>
> —**Naomi Watts,** English actress and producer, on her relationship with Heath Ledger

I was never one to patiently pick up broken fragments and glue them together again and tell myself that the mended whole was as good as new. What is broken is broken—and I'd rather remember it as it was at its best than mend it and see the broken places as long as I lived.

—**Margaret Mitchell,** journalist and author of Gone with The Wind

Real loss only occurs when you lose something that you love more than yourself.

—Unknown wild woman

It's a long road when you face the world alone, when no one reaches out a hand for you to hold. You can find love if you search within your soul, and the emptiness you felt will disappear.

—**Mariah Carey,** resilient chart-topping chanteuse

When It's Time to Get Lost

Sure, it hurts, but sometimes you just gotta cut somebody loose. Trust us, you'll feel better once it's done. Here are a few warning signs, courtesy of breakup and healing experts Marni Kamins and Janice MacLeod, authors of *The Breakup Repair Kit*.

- When you're making love, you'd rather be reading a magazine.

- Your eyes glaze over when he talks.

- He tells you things you don't agree with and you choose to ignore them.

- You know in your heart that if he wasn't paying for the meal, you'd rather be eating it with someone else.

- He's a dick to his mom—definitely a stop sign. How he treats his mother is how he will eventually treat you.

- You find yourself wondering if he gets skid marks in his underwear.

- And for those of you already dealing with a lost love, hang in there! Give yourself lots of TLC, and soon you'll be getting it from someone else again.

I wanted a perfect ending. Now I've learned the hard way that some poems don't rhyme, and some stories don't have a clear beginning, middle, and end. Life is about not knowing, having to change, taking the moment and making the best of it, without knowing what's going to happen next.

—**Gilda Radner,** SNL original cast member, comedian, and actress

Loneliness is a sign you are in desperate need of yourself.

—**Rupi Kaur,** Canadian poet, writer, illustrator, and performer

Love never dies a natural death. It dies because we don't know how to replenish its source. It dies of blindness and errors and betrayals. It dies of illness and wounds; it dies of weariness, of withering, of tarnishing.

—Anais Nin, erotic author extraordinaire

However often marriage is dissolved, it remains indissoluble. Real divorce, the divorce of heart and nerve and fiber, does not exist, since there is no divorce from memory.

—Virgilia Peterson, author and radio and TV personality

A divorce is like an amputation; you survive, but there's less of you.

—**Margaret Atwood,** Canadian literary critic, eco-activist, and author of The Handmaid's Tale

After all, my erstwhile dear,
my no longer cherished;
Need we say it was not love,
just because it perished?

—**Edna St. Vincent Millay,** renowned poet and playwright

I am done looking for love where it doesn't exist. I am done coughing up dust in attempts to drink from dry wells.

—**Maggie Georgiana Young,** adventuress and provocative feminist memoirist

If you love someone, let them go. If they return to you, it was meant to be. If they don't, their love was never yours to begin with.

—Unknown wild woman

When once estrangement has arisen between those who truly love each other, everything seems to widen the breach.

—**Mary Elizabeth Braddon,** popular English Victorian novelist, playwright, and editor

A bizarre sensation pervades a relationship of pretense. No truth seems true. A simple morning's greeting and response appear loaded with innuendo and fraught with implications. Each nicety becomes more sterile and each withdrawal more permanent.

—**Maya Angelou,** distinguished poet, memoirist, and civil rights activist

Two separate, distinct personalities, not separate at all, but inextricably bound, soul and body and mind, to each other; how did we get so far apart so fast?

—**Judith Guest,** novelist and screenwriter known for the Oscar-winning film *Ordinary People*

Badass Frida Kahlo:
Frida Forever!

Frida Kahlo's posthumous pop culture deification has eclipsed that of her husband, Mexican muralist Diego Rivera. A total iconoclast, Frida's visceral painting style has an intensity matched by few artists. Her fleshy fruits, torn arteries, tortured birthings, and imago-packed surrealist dreamscapes terrify and mesmerize. Her burning eyes in both self-portraiture and photographs make her hard to forget. Her pain seems to emanate from many wounds—psychic, physical, and romantic.

Born Magdalena Carmen Frida Kahlo y Calderon outside of Mexico City in 1907, her exotic looks, which mesmerized millions, were a product of her heritage. Frida's father, one of Mexico's preeminent photographers, was a first-generation Mexican born of Hungarian Jews, while her mother, Matilde Calderon, was a Mexican of mixed Spanish/Indian ancestry. Frida contracted polio when she was seven; though she survived, it stunted her right leg. Her father took charge of her recovery from polio, encouraging her to play sports to build back the strength of her right foot and leg. At fifteen, Frida was in a horrendous trolley-car accident that crushed her spine, right foot, and pelvis, leaving her crippled forever. Later, she depicted the crash as the loss of her virginity when the trolley car's handbrake pierced her young body. In pain for the remainder of her life, she underwent thirty-five surgeries, including the eventual amputation of her gangrenous right foot, and endured what she deemed as imprisonment when she was bedridden in body casts. Indeed, several of Kahlo's greatest works were done while flat on her back, using a special easel her mother had made for her.

Her tempestuous relationship with world-renowned painter Diego Rivera was also a source of great suffering. Often described as "froglike" in aspect, the Mexican art star was quite a ladies' man. During a hiatus in their marriage to each other, Frida hacked off her beautiful long hair and dressed in baggy men's suits. She bitterly rued her inability to bear Rivera a child and grieved over several miscarriages. They went about making art in very different ways—Rivera's huge paintings were political messages on the walls of public buildings; Frida's paintings were deeply personal, vibrant colored paintings often done on tiny pieces of tin.

Frida and Diego were a very public couple. Coming of age in the wake of the Mexican Revolution, they were both very political, and counted Leon Trotsky, Pablo Picasso, Russian filmmaker Sergei Einstein, Andre Breton, and the Rockefellers among their friends. Both artists embraced "Mexicanismo," Frida going so far as to wear traditional Indian peasant costumes at all times, cutting a striking and memorable figure with the rustic formality. Frida's stalwart adherence to all things "of the people" made her a national shero, with papers commenting on her resemblance to an Indian princess or goddess. In his article, "Portrait of Frida Kahlo as Tehuana," art critic Hayden Herrera asserts that the Latina artist was "unrestrained by her native Mexico's male-dominated culture.

Tehuantepec women are famous for being stately, beautiful, smart, brave, and strong; according to legend, theirs is a matriarchal society where women run the markets, handle fiscal matters, and dominate the men."

More than forty years after her death, Frida and her work hold a fascination that shows no sign of fading. Her dramatic personal style and wild paintings have captured the public's imagination. She has been hailed as a role model for women artists, as well as a stylistic pioneer and idealist who pursued her craft despite physical handicaps that would have stopped many others. Her body was broken, but her spirit was indomitable, like the Tehuana women she identified with. As Herrera notes, "She became famous for her heroic '*allegria*.' "

Falling out of love is chiefly a matter of forgetting how charming someone is.

—Iris Murdoch, Anglo-Irish novelist and philosopher

How lucky I am to have known someone so hard to say goodbye to.

—Unknown wild woman

If we deny love that is given to us, if we refuse to give love because we fear the pain of loss, then our lives will be empty, our loss greater.

—**Margaret Weis** and **Tracy Hickman,** fantasy authors and creators of the *Dragonlance* game world

> *Only when you are lost can love find itself in you without losing its way.*
>
> **—Hélène Cixous,** French literary critic, professor, playwright, poet, and feminist writer

> *A broken heart is what makes life so wonderful—five years later.*
>
> **—Phyllis Battelle,** sardonic reporter and author

> *Some people think that it's holding on that makes one strong; sometimes it's letting go.*
>
> **—Sylvia Robinson,** singer, musician, producer, and founder of Sugar Hill Records

Parrots, tortoises, and redwoods live a longer life than men do; men a longer life than dogs do; dogs a longer life than love does.

—**Edna St. Vincent Millay,** renowned poet and playwright

If love means that one person absorbs the other, then no real relationship exists any more. Love evaporates; there is nothing left to love. The integrity of self is gone.

—**Ann Oakley,** distinguished British sociologist, feminist, and writer

We who were loved will never unlive that crippling fever.

—**Adrienne Rich,** acclaimed poet, essayist, and radical feminist

Love is the direct opposite of hate. By definition it's something you can't feel for more than a few minutes at a time, so what's all this bullshit about loving somebody for the rest of your life?

—**Judith Rossner,** bestselling novelist of Looking for Mr. Goodbar and August

CHAPTER 5

•

Do We Really Even Need Men Anymore?

For a long time, I thought I wanted to be a nun. Then I realized that what I really wanted to be was a lesbian.

—**Mabel Maney,** artist, author, and creator of the Nancy Clue and the Hardly Boys and Jane Bond parody series

Free love? As if love is anything but free! Man has bought brains, but all the millions in the world have failed to buy love. Man has subdued bodies, but all the power on earth has been unable to subdue love. Man has conquered and fettered the spirit, but he has been utterly helpless before love. High on a throne with all the splendor and pomp his gold can command, man is yet poor and desolate, if love passes him by. And if it stays, the poorest hovel is radiant with warmth, with life and color. Thus, love has the magic power to make of a beggar a king. Yes, love is free; it can dwell in no other atmosphere.

—**Emma Goldman,** anarchist feminist activist, philosopher, and writer

What do you mean, you "don't believe in homosexuality"? It's not like the Easter Bunny, your belief isn't necessary.

—**Lea DeLaria,** proud comedian, actor, and jazz musician

I believed that the best way to get to know a woman was to go to bed with her...so pretty much everywhere I've lived I've had a real bad reputation. But it has gotten me a lot of interesting dates.

—**Dorothy Allison,** provocative bestselling lesbian author

I've had long-term sexual relationships with both men and women. If that classifies me as bisexual, then I'm bisexual.

—**Sandra Bernhard,** snarky actress, comedian, singer, and author

Tell someone close to you how much you love them, even if you're sure they already know.

—Becca Badass Anderson

The infantile needs of adult men for women have been sentimentalized and romanticized long enough as "love"; it is time to recognize them as arrested development.

—**Adrienne Rich,** acclaimed poet, essayist, and radical feminist

If love is the answer, could you rephrase the question?

—**Lily Tomlin,** inspired lesbian actress, comedian, writer, singer, and producer

For her, and her alone, I could have been a lesbian.

—actress and diva **Joan Crawford** going on about Greta Garbo

My lesbianism is an act of Christian charity. All those women out there praying for a man, and I'm giving them my share.

—**Rita Mae Brown,** pioneering lesbian author

In itself, homosexuality is as limiting as heterosexuality: the ideal should be to be capable of loving a woman or a man; either, a human being, without feeling fear, restraint, or obligation.

—**Simone de Beauvoir,** intellectual, writer, philosopher, and social theorist

Badass Sappho: The Love That Dared to Speak Its Name

Lyric poet Sappho is widely regarded as the greatest writer of ancient times. She came to be known as the "tenth muse." While scholars can't agree whether Homer even existed, Sappho's work was recorded and preserved by other writers. Although she is believed to have been married and had one daughter, much of her work is written to other women, exalting them for their beauty and often achieving a poetic frenzy of desire. She also makes references to the political arena of the ancient world she inhabited.

The unfortunate destruction of a volume of all her work—nine books of lyric poetry and one of elegiac verse—occurred in the early Middle yAges, engendering a search for her writing that continues even now. The Catholic Church deemed her poetry to be obscene and burned the only volume containing her complete body of work, thus erasing what could only be some of the finest poetry in all of history. Known for its powerful phrasing and intensity of feeling, erotic and otherwise, Sappho's poetry is immediately striking and accessible to the reader. Upon reading Sappho, you feel that you know her; her ecstatic expressions of lesbian passion still inspire, and she is regarded stylistically as being the first modern poet.

O soft and dainty maiden, from afar
I watch you, as amidst the flowers you move,
And pluck them, singing.
More golden than all gold your tresses are:
Never was harp-note like your voice, my love,
Your voice sweet-ringing.

—**Sappho** of Lesbos

My mom blames California for me being
a lesbian. "Everything was fine until you
moved out there." "That's right, Mom, we have
mandatory lesbianism in west Hollywood. The
Gay Patrol busted me, and I was given seven
business days to add a significant amount of
flannel to my wardrobe."

—**Coley Sohn,** funny lesbian stage & screen actress and
indie filmmaker

We love men. We just don't want to see them naked.

—Two Nice Girls, "dyke rock" band out of Austin, Texas

When you're in love, you never really know whether your elation comes from the qualities of the one you love, or if it attributes them to her; whether the light which surrounds her like a halo comes from you, from her, or from the meeting of your sparks.

—Natalie Clifford Barney, American expatriate playwright, poet, novelist, and Parisian salonist

Every woman I have ever loved has left her print upon me, where I loved some invaluable piece of myself apart from me—so different that I had to stretch and grow in order to recognize her. And in that growing, we came to separation, that place where work begins.

—**Audre Lorde,** award-winning writer, poet, and civil rights activist

I was raised around heterosexuals...that's where us gay people come from.

—**Ellen DeGeneres,** comedian, writer, producer, actor, and awards and talk show host

I can play a heterosexual. I know how they walk. I know how they talk. You don't have to be one to play one.

—**Lily Tomlin,** insightful lesbian actress, comedian, writer, singer, and producer

Are there many things in this cool-hearted world so utterly exquisite as the pure love of one woman for another?

—**Mary MacLane,** pioneering and controversial turn-of-the-century memoirist

Hick darling...I couldn't say "je t'aime et je t'adore" as I longed to do, but always remember I am saying it, that I sleep thinking of you.

—**Eleanor Roosevelt,** social activist FLOTUS of the '30s and '40s, in a letter to Lorena Hickok

Badass Pop Culture Power Couples

Lesbians, bisexuals, and non-straight women of all types have been around forever, from the literary world to the high seas. Just take a look at this extremely abbreviated list of famous devoted ladies!

- Willa Cather, an American writer
- Edith Lewis, a magazine editor
- Gertrude Stein, author and poet
- Alice B. Toklas, author

- Katharine Lee Bates, poet and Wellesley College professor (who incidentally wrote the poem "America the Beautiful")

- Katharine Coman, Wellesley College dean

- Angelina Weld Grimke, author and famed abolitionist

- Mamie Burrill, playwright, director, actor, and teacher

- Sara Teasdale, poet

- Susan Sontag, author and critic

- Annie Liebovitz, portrait photographer of renown

- Lady Eleanor Butler and Sarah Ponsonby, eighteenth-century Brits (*The General Evening Post* referred to them as the "Ladies of Llangeollen" in 1790)

- Anne Cormac Bonny and Mary Read, pirates (These two outlaws were brought to trial in 1720.)

I'm a "trisexual." I'll try anything once.

—**Samantha** (played by actress Kim Cattrall) on Sex and the City

What is a lesbian? A lesbian is a woman who loves women, who counts on women for emotional support, who looks to women for her growth, who finds her identity in her womanhood. A lesbian is a woman who more and more willingly, and with more and more pride, knows and shows her own strength, makes her own definitions for herself, and dares to defy society's most sacred taboo—"Thou shalt not live without men and like it."

—**Ginny Berson** and **Robin Brooks,** founders of pioneering women's music label Olivia Records

We women are the best thing going—we are warm, passionate, we cry, and we live! Let's celebrate!

—**Margaret Sloan-Hunter,** African-American lesbian feminist civil rights advocate and Ms. editor

Poetry is the conflict in the lives we lead. It is the most subversive because it is in the business of encouraging change.

—**Audre Lorde**

But I always have and still do consider myself queer. To me, being queer isn't who you're sleeping with; it's just an idea that sexuality isn't gender-based, that it's love-based.

—**Ani DiFranco,** singer, songwriter, multi-instrumentalist, and feminist icon, in response to criticism for loving a male

I wear a T-shirt that says, "The family tree stops here."

—**Suzanne Westenhoefer,** proud lesbian comedian

Pronouns make it hard to keep our sexual orientation a secret when our coworkers ask us about our weekend. "I had a great time with...them." Great! Now they don't think you're queer—just a big slut!

—**Judy Carter,** lesbian comic

My father warned me about men and booze, but he never mentioned a word about women and cocaine.

—**Tallulah Bankhead,** adventurous actress and famously witty woman

Cut the ending. Revise the script. The man of her dreams is a girl.

—**Julie Anne Peters,** young adult fiction author of *Keeping You a Secret*

A Badass Celebration: Happy Galentine's Day!!

Galentine's Day. It isn't a widely celebrated holiday, few could even place it on a calendar. But, despite not being widely known, it is a very important holiday. Celebrated the day before the most romantic holiday of the year, Galentine's Day is a day for all ladies to thank and appreciate the wonderful girlfriends they have in their lives. Created on the TV show *Parks and Recreation* by the show's main protagonist Leslie Knope, the true meaning of Galentine's Day can be summed up with these words: "It's only the best day of the year. Every February 13, my lady friends and I leave our husbands and our boyfriends at home, and we just come and kick it, breakfast-style. Ladies celebrating ladies."

Badass women become their best selves when surrounded by other women who support them. Why wouldn't we celebrate that? A little chocolate, a card with a heart on it—why only save these for a significant other? I say share a little bit of that love with your best friends and let them know how much you appreciate them being in your life.

In this spread, you will find quotes from some of the best and baddest women around. From the silver screen to reality TV, these women range widely across the badass spectrum. The one thing they all have in common: they know the true value of having great girlfriends.

You know when I feel inwardly beautiful? When I am with my girlfriends and we are having a "goddess circle."

—**Jennifer Aniston,** actress and producer

I don't know what I would have done so many times in my life if I hadn't had my girlfriends.

—**Reese Witherspoon,** actress, producer,
and entrepreneur

If you can find a group of women, any age, who are supportive and kind and love you, that's the best. I have a group of girlfriends that I would lie in front of a bus for. They've picked me up through really, really bad times and I can definitely say I've done the same for them.

—**Katie Lowes,** actress and theatrical director

We're getting ready to take over the world. My group of girlfriends—we're renegades.

—**Lisa Bonet,** television and film actress

I have a reputation for being cold and aloof, but I'm so not that woman. I'm passionate. I love my girls, being with my girlfriends, getting involved with issues that affect other women and children who are suffering.

—Annie Lennox, Scottish musician, activist, and philanthropist

Whether you're throwing up or breaking up, you want your girlfriend right there! I don't trust women who don't go to their girlfriends.

—Drew Barrymore, actress, director, and producer

I think that it's really important to have good friends. Nowadays, you can text 24 hours a day and be in constant contact, but every once in a while, it's nice to just get out with your girlfriends and have fun.

—**Amanda Schull,** actress and former ballet dancer

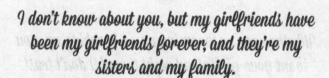

I don't know about you, but my girlfriends have been my girlfriends forever, and they're my sisters and my family.

—**Elizabeth Olsen,** actress and sister of the famous Olsen twins

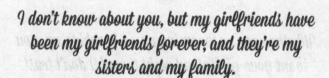

Oh my God, my girlfriends are everything to me. They celebrate with you, they cry with you, they hold you when you need to be held. They laugh with you. They're mean with you! They're always there, and it's just a priceless thing to have.

—**Jennifer Lopez,** singer, dancer, and fashion designer

The only people you can really share certain things with in secret are your girlfriends.

—**Shirley Knight,** veteran actress of stage and screen

I still have friends from primary school. And my two best girlfriends are from secondary school. I don't have to explain anything to them. I don't have to apologize for anything. They know. There's no judgment in any way.

—**Emma Watson,** actress, model, and activist

Men come and go—God knows they certainly have in my life—but girlfriends are forever. I have a lot of girlfriends but only a few very, very close ones.

—**Alana Stewart,** actress and model

I think that is one reason why women live longer than men. Friendship between women is different than friendship between men. We talk about different things. We delve deep. We go under, even if we haven't seen each other for years.... It's my women friends that keep starch in my spine, and without them, I don't know where I would be. We have to just hang together and help each other.

—**Jane Fonda,** actress, fitness entrepreneur, and activist

Abandon the cultural myth that all female friendships must be bitchy, toxic, or competitive. This myth is like heels and purses—pretty but designed to SLOW women down.

—**Roxane Gay,** writer, editor, and professor

As hard as it is and as tired as I am, I force myself to get dinner at least once a week with my girlfriends or have a sleepover. Otherwise my life is just work.

—Jennifer Lawrence, highest-paid actress in the world

Once a month, I get together with my girlfriends, and we usually check into a hotel or go to someone else's house. We can talk for fifteen hours, and it just flies by.

—Leslie Mann, comedian and actress

It's important to have girlfriends, because guys tend to come and go.

—Ashley Tisdale, actress, singer, and producer

CHAPTER 6

•

*Strong Women,
Strong Coffee,
Strong Love*

Staying at home is simply not a luxury or even a desire many of us have anymore. In most women's lives, the housewife is no more. Instead, working has become the mainstay of our existences. Whether that work is as a doctor, a teacher, or a police officer, we women know what it's like to fight to succeed and make a name for ourselves in the workplace.

Whether in fields that are filled with men or in a field that doesn't pay much, we still toil nine to five (or more likely these days, eight to six) just to keep body and soul together. And even if we're lucky enough to labor with love, we'll probably spend most days of our adult lives engaged in work of one sort or another. (On the bright side, at least as employed grownups we don't have anyone telling us we can't have ice cream whenever we want.)

This chapter, then, is for everyone. For those who haven't yet discovered a gratifying way to earn their daily bread. (How about Congress? Maybe professional taste-testing?) For those who are curious to know how other women get through the work day. (With pleasure, with passion, with heaping amounts of caffeine.) For those who harbor dire suspicions about the flip side of success. (Ready for speculation about your sexual preference, Ms. Overachiever?) And for those who are at work

right this minute, looking for some semblance of a distraction from boredom.

A woman is like a teabag—you can't tell how strong she is until you put her in hot water.

—Eleanor Roosevelt, fearless FLOTUS, activist, politician, and diplomat

If you want something said, ask a man; if you want something done, ask a woman.

—Margaret Thatcher, British stateswoman

How wrong it is for a woman to expect the man to build the world she wants, rather than to create it herself.

—**Anais Nin,** empowered diarist and erotica author

I want Vogue to be smart, sharp, and sexy—I'm not interested in the super-rich or infinitely leisured. I want our readers to be energetic executive women with money of their own and a wide range of interests. There is a new kind of woman out there. She's interested in business and money.

—**Anna Wintour,** killer queen of fashion magazines

I do not wish women to have power over men;
but to have power over themselves.

—Mary Shelley, famed nineteenth century author
of *Frankenstein*

Women are the largest untapped reservoir of
talent in the world.

—Hillary Clinton, U.S. stateswoman

Women who stay true to themselves are always more interesting and beautiful to me: women like Frida Kahlo, Georgia O'Keeffe, and Anna Magnani—women who have style, chic, allure and elegance. They didn't submit to any standard of beauty—they defined it.

—**Isabella Rossellini,** filmmaker, actress, author, and philanthropist

Toughness doesn't have to come in a pinstripe suit.

—**Dianne Feinstein,** U.S. Senator since 1992

Rest and you rust.

—**Helen Hayes,** prize-winning twentieth century actress

A Badass Woman's Place is On Top (of a Mountain!)

Fifty years earlier, Arlene Blum would not have been allowed into certain areas in the Great Himalayan range. It was an entirely different kind of explorer who helped open those gates. In 1924, spiritual seeker Alexandra David-Neel was the first western woman to visit Tibet's "Forbidden City," Lhasa, in its mountain perch. Dressed as a beggar and traveling so light that they didn't even have blankets, the fifty-five-year-old Alexandra and a young monk made the perilous climb up 18,000 feet to the holy city. Her travelogue is one of the most treasured resources in Asian studies, published as *My Journey to Lhasa*.

Opera singer turned scholar, the intrepid Frenchwoman also has the honor of being the first western woman to have had an audience with the Dalai Lama during his exile in India.

Alexandra never did anything halfway, and she found the study of Buddhism so appealing that she moved into an ascetic's snowy cave, where she undertook the studies and spiritual practice of a Buddhist nun. She became such an adept that she reportedly was able to control her body temperature through meditation, and there are legends of levitation and other psychic phenomenon. Pooh-poohing the supernatural, her explanation for these matters is simple and practical: she learned from the Tibetans that it is all a matter of management of natural energies. One of the world's earliest scholars in Eastern Studies and Oriental mysticism, Alexandra David-Neel's unique combination of daring and curiosity made her one of the most fascinating women in any part of the world.

Then there's Lynn Hill. Although many of our sports-sheroes have made strides for women simply by being the best, others, like Lynn Hill, have done so with great intention. Lynn Hill is a world-class climber whose stated mission is to create equality for women climbers in an admittedly steep arena. In what was previously a totally male-dominated sport requiring strength women "aren't supposed to have," Lynn Hill rocketed to the top, demanding to be allowed to climb as well as any man. As she says, "If extreme athletics improves you as a person, why can't that be feminine?"

And don't forget Annie Smith Peck. She was a classical scholar born in 1850 with a yen for heights. Wearing a suit of animal skins explorer Robert Edwin Peary had brought back from his exploration of the Arctic Circle, she climbed the Andean apex of Mount Huascaran and went on to become the foremost female mountain climber of her day. She was fifty-eight years old at the time. She wrote about her exploits and became quite a popular travel writer. One of her most sheroic exploits involved climbing the formidable Mount Coropuna in Peru and hanging a banner at the summit reading, "Votes for Women!" She didn't stop climbing until a year before her death at age eighty-five.

We are coming down from our pedestal and up from the laundry room.

—**Bella Abzug,** famed U.S. Congresswoman
and activist

Whatever you do, be different—that was the advice my mother gave me, and I can't think of better advice for an entrepreneur. If you're different, you will stand out.

—**Anita Roddick,** activist and entrepreneur founder of
The Body Shop

A lot of people are afraid to say what they want. That's why they don't get what they want.

—**Madonna,** iconic performer

The question isn't who's going to let me; it's who is going to stop me.

—**Ayn Rand,** writer and Objectivist philosopher

Badass Mamahood and Running a Household (or Not!)

Motherhood doesn't begin easily. Instead, it starts more along the lines of a "give me morphine and get this out of me" experience. Growing and ejecting a seven-pound baby requires the machismo of a Hemingway hero, and at least the valor of Superman. But it doesn't end at the birth—while the next eighteen years might not require as much physical effort, they will require enough emotional stamina to take care of a small village.

And having children does not constitute an excuse for lazing around, performing tasks like keeping said offspring alive and out of jail. No, Modern Moms labor (metaphorically or otherwise) continuously to get the title of "having it all." Why not have a family and travel the world, convert all farms to non-GMO produce, or organize a presidential campaign? Why not make a trio of healthy, kid-pleasing meals every day—while of course still maintaining your campaign and other side interests? Well, there's no reason to believe it's impossible. Especially if you are the kind of parent that not only has children, but spends time with them.

Of course, we love our children, despite the all-encompassing chaos they introduce into our lives. (They're especially dear when they're asleep.) In general, I believe we're also fond of our homes. But there isn't a woman alive who'll tell you that the domestic goddess gig is a breeze. For a little advice and encouragement from the women who have been there and done that, read on.

I was raised to be an independent woman, not the victim of anything.

—**Kamala Harris,** U.S. politician

When God created man and woman, he was thinking, "Who shall I give the power to, to give birth to the next human being?" And God chose woman. And this is the big evidence that women are powerful.

—**Malala Yousafzai,** death-defying education activist and youngest ever Nobel prize winner

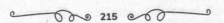

Any woman who understands the problems of running a home will be nearer to understanding the problems of running a country

—**Margaret Thatcher,** British stateswoman

I think as a woman it's in our nature to nurture someone else. Sometimes at the expense of ourselves.

—**Emilia Clarke,** English actress

It may be the cock that crows, but it is the hen that lays the eggs.

—**Margaret Thatcher,** British prime minister 1979–1990

I am an example of what is possible when girls from the very beginning of their lives are loved and nurtured by people around them. I was surrounded by extraordinary women in my life who taught me about quiet strength and dignity.

—**Michelle Obama,** attorney, writer, and U.S. First Lady 2009–2017

Because sorry to say, women run the house. They run the family. They hold things up. I mean, it's like you don't ever see your mom get sick because she handles everything. And it's kind of amazing, I think, to show people just how strong women are.

—**Sophia Bush,** actress, director, and activist

There are practical little things in housekeeping which no man really understands.

—**Eleanor Roosevelt,** U.S. politician and activist FLOTUS

~~Housekeeping ain't no joke.~~

—**Hannah,** servant in Louisa May Alcott's groundbreaking women's novel, *Little Women*

Child-rearing can be a tedious and thankless undertaking.

—**Jessica Valenti,** feminist writer and blogger

The natural state of motherhood is unselfishness. When you become a mother, you are no longer the center of your own universe. You relinquish that position to your children.

—Jessica Lange, acclaimed actress

Sometimes the strength of motherhood is greater than natural laws.

—Barbara Kingsolver, prize-winning writer and poet

Motherhood is tough. If you just want a wonderful little creature to love, you can get a puppy.

—Barbara Walters, American broadcast journalist, talk show host, and author

Parents can only give good advice or put them [children] on the right paths, but the final forming of a person's character lies in their own hands.

—**Anne Frank,** world-renowned German diarist

A woman is the full circle. Within her is the power to create, nurture, and transform.

—**Diane Mariechild,** feminist author

My honor was not yielded, but conquered merely.

—**Cleopatra,** last ruling pharaoh of the Ptolemaic Kingdom of Egypt

No husband of mine will say, "I could have been a drummer, but I had to think about the wife and kids. You know how it is." Nobody supports me at the expense of his own adventure.

—**Maxine Hong Kingston,** Asian-American author and wise woman

Ted needs someone to be there one hundred percent of the time. He thinks that's love. It's not love—it's babysitting.

—**Jane Fonda,** actress, fitness entrepreneur, and activist

I don't want to say that I want a man to like me for my mind, because that's going to sound like I think I'm Albert Einstein. But I would like someone who doesn't accuse me of making up words like "segue."

—Mariah Carey, resilient chart-topping chanteuse

Better an old man's darling than a young man's slave.

—Alberta Martin, the "Oldest Living Confederate Widow," who married a man sixty years her senior

Basically, I've dodged that marriage bullet...I like the jewelry part of getting married, but I can buy my own damn rings, too.

—**Queen Latifah,** royal rap star, actress, talk show host, and TV and record producer

Men are always ready to respect anything that bores them.

—**Marilyn Monroe,** iconic blond bombshell actress and singer

It is no longer obligatory upon a woman to give herself to one man to save herself from being torn to pieces by the rest.

—**Jane Cunningham Croly,** journalist and pioneering author and editor of women's columns

> *The fantasy that we are overwhelmed by Rhett Butler should be traded in for one in which we seize state power and reeducate him.*

—**Sandra Lee Bartky,** philosophy and gender studies professor

> *Scratch most feminists and underneath there is a woman who longs to be a sex object. The difference is that is not all she wants to be.*

—**Betty Rollin,** TV correspondent, author, and breast cancer expert

> *My scars teach me that I am stronger than what caused them.*
>
> —**Manal Al-Sharif,** Daring to Drive: A Saudi Woman's Awakening

> *Trouble is part of your life—if you don't share it, you don't give the person who loves you a chance to love you enough.*
>
> —**Dinah Shore,** chart-topping mid-century singer, actress, and talk show host

Badass Amazon Penthesilea: Wonder Woman's Gal Pal

The daughter of Orithia, Penthesilea was the ruler of Amazonia, a Bronze Age nation near the Black Sea. Considered the greatest Amazon of all times, she was a fierce warrior; her name means "compelling men to mourn." Although the nation of Amazonia itself was peaceful and self-sufficient, its women warriors were regarded as the most highly skilled soldiers in the world. Even the Argonauts, the piratical adventurers of myth, dropped their plans to invade Amazonia after observing the strength of its army.

Penthesilea's zeal for battle was fueled by her grief and rage after the death of her sister. At the request of Queen Hecuba, she liberated the city of Troy, which had been under siege by the Greeks for years. Many scholars believe that Homer adapted his famous story of the Trojan War from an account by the Egyptian poetess Phantasia, rewriting it to cater to the patriarchal tastes of his Greek audience. The consensus among herstorians is that Penthesilea crossed swords with Achilles during the war and that the great Greek warrior fell deeply in love with her. Differing versions of the legend depict her alternately as either the victor or the slain in the duel, but all agree she proved

to be the only soldier Achilles ever encountered who was his equal.

We can do no great things; only small things with great love.

—**Mother Teresa,** philanthropic missionary nun

It is really asking too much of a woman to expect her to bring up her husband and her children too.

—**Lillian Bell,** wild woman writer

Him that I love, I wish to be free—even from me.

—Anne Morrow Lindbergh, author, journalist, and aviator

You don't have to be anti-man to be pro-woman.

—Jane Galvin Lewis, comedian and founder of the National Black Feminist Organization

The best friend you have is you.

—Carol Wiseman, comforting advice author

Friendship with oneself is all-important, because without it, one cannot be friends with anybody else in the world.

—Eleanor Roosevelt, self-assured activist, politician, and fearless FLOTUS

I have an everyday religion that works for me. Love yourself first, and everything else falls into line.

—Lucille Ball, comic, actress, producer, and film-studio executive

*I love people. I love my family, my children...
but inside myself is a place where I live all
alone, and that's where you renew your springs
that never dry up.*

—**Pearl S. Buck,** author and Nobel Prize winner

*People, even more than things, have to be
restored, renewed, revived, reclaimed, and
redeemed; never throw out anyone.*

—**Audrey Hepburn,** piquant actress, dancer,
and humanitarian

*No person is your friend who demands your
silence, or denies your right to grow.*

—**Alice Walker,** award-winning author, poet, and activist

The love of our neighbor in all its fullness simply means being able to say, "What are you going through?"

—**Simone Weil,** French philosopher, activist, and Christian mystic

I'd kiss a frog even if there was no promise of a Prince Charming popping out of it. I love frogs.

—**Cameron Diaz,** actress, comedienne, and producer

> *I think the reason we're so crazy sexually in America is that all our responses are acting. We don't know how to feel. We know how it looked in the movies.*

—Jill Robinson, trend-tracking writer

Gal Pals, Badass BFF's, and Good Friends: Our Other Significant Others

Any wild woman knows that her lovers aren't the only people in her life who deserve love and devotion. Here's to the women who stand by us when we really need it—our friends.

We move forward when we realize how resilient and striking the women around us are.

—**Rupi Kaur,** Canadian poet, writer, illustrator, and performer

One friend with whom you have a lot in common is better than three with whom you struggle to find things to talk about. We never needed best friend gear, because I guess with real friends you don't have to make it official. It just is.

—**Mindy Kaling,** actress, comedian, and writer

The most beautiful discovery that true friends can make is that you can grow separately without growing apart.

—**Elizabeth Foley,** angel healer and psychic development teacher

We're connected, as women. It's like a spiderweb. If one part of that web vibrates, if there's trouble, we all know it, but most of the time we're just too scared, or selfish, or insecure to help. But if we don't help each other, who will?

—**Sarah Addison Allen,** bestselling author of The Peach Keeper

A friend is someone who knows all about you and loves you anyway!

—**Leslie Rossman,** wise woman and power publicist

You don't make friends, you earn them!

—**Deena Patel Wine,** justice-minded legal lady

I can trust my friends. These people force me to examine and encourage me to grow.

—**Cher,** iconic pop singer and actress

A friend is someone who knows the song in your heart and can sing it back to you when you have forgotten the words.

—**Shania Twain,** bestselling female country singer/songwriter

If you judge people, you have no time to love them.

—**Mother Teresa,** philanthropic missionary nun

A real friend is one who walks in when the rest of the world walks out.

—**Beth Bachtold,** insightful writer

The sharing of joy, whether physical, emotional, psychic, or intellectual, forms a bridge between the sharers which can be the basis for understanding much of what is not shared between them, and lessens the threat of their difference.

—**Audre Lorde,** award-winning writer, poet, and civil rights activist

I always felt that the great high privilege, relief, and comfort of friendship was that one had to explain nothing.

—**Katherine Mansfield,** prominent short fiction author

We all need friends with whom we speak of our deepest concerns and who do not fear to speak the truth in love to us.

—**Margaret Guenther,** author, Episcopal priest, and seminary professor

Though friendship is not quick to burn, it is explosive stuff.

—**May Sarton,** poet, novelist, and memoirist

When one is out of touch with oneself, one cannot touch others.

—**Anne Morrow Lindbergh,** author, journalist, and aviator

It seems to me that trying to live without friends is like milking a bear to get cream for your morning coffee. It is a whole lot of trouble, and then not worth much after you get it.

—**Zora Neale Hurston,** novelist, folklorist, and anthropologist

Friendship is the finest balm for the pangs of despised love.

—**Jane Austen,** classic novelist known for social commentary

Women of my generation, unlike generations before us, we have been with several men—or in some cases, many men. I raise the question, why?

—**Joni Mitchell,** generation-defining singer-songwriter

Self-help books are making life downright unsafe. Women desperate to catch a man practice all the ploys recommended by these authors. Bump into him, trip over him, knock him down, spill something on him, scald him, but meet him.

—**Florence King,** acerbically witty and misanthropic writer and columnist

Nothing melts a woman's heart like gold.

—Susannah Centlivre, poet, actress, and the most successful playwright of the eighteenth century

I wanted to make it really special on Valentine's Day, so I tied my boyfriend up. And for three solid hours I watched whatever I wanted to on TV.

—Tracy Smith, comedienne and writer

The most important thing in a relationship between a man and a woman is that one of them must be good at taking orders.

—Linda Festa, witty epigrammist

Women have one great advantage over men. It is commonly thought that if they marry, they have done enough and need career no further. If a man marries, on the other hand, public opinion is all against him if he takes this view.

—**Dame Rose Macaulay,** award-winning novelist

These are very confusing times. For the first time in history a woman is expected to combine intelligence with a sharp hairdo, a raised consciousness with high heels, and an open, nonsexist relationship with a tan guy who has a great bod.

—**Lynda Barry,** feminist cartoonist, author, and teacher

The ultimate test of a relationship is to disagree
but to hold hands.

—**Alexandra Penney,** women's author, editor, artist,
and journalist

Men who consistently leave the toilet seat up
secretly want women to get up to go to the
bathroom in the middle of the night and fall in.

—**Rita Rudner,** famed stand-up comedienne

Maybe I've been married a few too many
times. I love a good party, but I have recently
realized that I can actually just throw a party
and not get married.

—**Whoopi Goldberg,** comedian, actress, and talk
show host

> **Behind every successful man is a surprised woman.**

—**Maryon Pearson,** Canadian known as a wellspring of wit

> **If you want to say it with flowers, a single rose says: "I'm cheap!"**

—**Delta Burke,** actress and producer

> **In real love, you want the other person's good. In romantic love, you want the other person.**

—**Margaret C. Anderson,** literary magazine founder, editor, and publisher

I love humanity, but I hate people.

—Edna St. Vincent Millay, renowned poet
and playwright

No one can understand love who has not experienced infatuation. And no one can understand infatuation, no matter how many times [s]he has experienced it.

—Mignon McLaughlin, journalist and author of The
Neurotic's Notebook and sequels

Every one of us needs to show how much we care for each other, and in the process, care for ourselves.

—Diana, Princess of Wales

Everyone admits that love is wonderful and necessary, yet no one agrees on just what it is.

—**Diane Ackerman,** poet, essayist, and naturalist

You can't put a price tag on love, but you can on all its accessories.

—**Melanie Clark Pullen,** Irish actress, producer, and writer

Love is a fire. But whether it is going to warm your hearth or burn down your house, you can never tell.

—**Joan Crawford,** classic grande dame actress of film and television

If one doesn't respect oneself, one can have neither love nor respect for others.

—**Ayn Rand,** writer and Objectivist philosopher

The ultimate lesson all of us have to learn is unconditional love, which includes not only others but ourselves as well.

—**Elizabeth Kubler-Ross,** pioneering Swiss-American psychiatrist and writer

A woman's love is a man's privilege, not his right.

—Unknown wild woman

Laugh, and the world laughs with you. Cry, and you cry with your girlfriends.

—**Laurie Kuslansky,** insightful writer

Start living now. Stop saving the good china for the special occasion. Stop withholding your love until that special person materializes. Every day you're alive is a special occasion. Every minute, every breath, is a gift from God.

—**Mary Manin Morrissey,** motivational speaker.

Just don't give up trying to do what you really want to do. Where there is love and inspiration, I don't think you can go wrong.

—**Ella Fitzgerald,** legendary singer known as the "Queen of Jazz"

I don't know about you, but I am glad my sweetheart is not a mind reader.

—**Mary Jane Ryan,** bestselling author and executive coach

Love is what we were born with. Fear is what we learned here.

—**Marianne Williamson,** spiritual teacher and author

Women measure their achievements not in the wealth they have gathered, but in the love they have gathered around them.

—**Linda MacFarlane,** reflective author

Not in strength are we inferior to men; the same our eyes, our limbs the same; one common light we see, one air we breathe; no different is the food we eat. What then denied to us hath heaven on man bestowed?

—Penthesilea, Amazon warrior queen

Badass Suffragettes Susan B. Anthony and Elizabeth Cady Stanton: Feminist Foremothers

Susan B. Anthony, the pioneer crusader for women's right to vote, was a precocious child. Raised in the 1820s by a Quaker father who believed in independent thinking and education for women, Susan learned to read and write by the time she was three. Her first career was as a schoolteacher, but she soon found her niche as a political reformer, taking up the cause of temperance, then abolition. In 1869, she and Elizabeth Cady Stanton organized the National Women's Suffrage Association and put out a pro-feminist paper, *The Revolution*.

When the Fourteenth Amendment to the Constitution was passed in 1872 guaranteeing equal rights for African-Americans, including the right as citizens to vote, Anthony and Stanton kicked into action, demanding the right to vote for women as well. Susan and a dozen other suffragists were jailed for trying to vote in the presidential election of that year. Undeterred, they began to work for a separate amendment giving this right to women. However, Congress patently ignored the amendments put before them each year on the vote for women until fifty years later.

Both Stanton and Anthony were real hell-raisers. Stanton, along with Lucretia Mott, organized the first women's rights convention in 1848 with a platform supporting women's rights to property, equal pay for equal work, and the right to vote. Stanton was introduced to Susan B. Anthony three years later. They were a "dream team" combination of Elizabeth's political theories and her ability to rouse people's emotions with Susan's unmatched skill as a logician and organizer par excellence. They founded the first temperance society for women and amazed everyone with their drastic call for drunkenness to be recognized as a legal basis for divorce. Reviled during her lifetime, Susan learned to live with the taunts and heckles; critics claimed that among other traits, she had "the proportions of a file and the voice of a hurdy-gurdy." Nonetheless, the "Napoleon" of the women's rights movement, as William Henry Channing called her, tirelessly lectured around the country for women's rights until her dying day in 1906. Although she didn't get to realize her dream of voting rights for women in her lifetime, the successors she and Stanton did finally win this landmark victory for the women of America. Of the 260 women who attended the foremothers' historic first women's rights convention in 1848, only one woman lived long enough to see the passing of the victorious 1920 amendment granting women the right to vote—

Charlotte Woodward. She declared at the time, "We little dreamed when we began this context that half a century later we would be compelled to leave the finish of the battle to another generation of women. But our hearts are filled with joy to know that they enter this task equipped with a college education, with business experience, with the freely admitted right to speak in public—all of which were denied to women fifty years ago."

Failure is impossible.

—**Susan B. Anthony,** women's rights activist and social reformer

Badasses Breaking the
Concrete Ceiling

Lucretia Mott worked with Elizabeth Cady Stanton in planning the Seneca Falls Convention. Mott was an electrifying speaker coming from Europe, where she was a well-known Quaker preacher. She didn't mince words and spoke powerfully and directly to women's rights, adding the radical note needed to light the fires of equal rights and abolition, "The world has never seen a truly great and virtuous nation, because in the degradation of women, the very foundations of life are poisoned at the source."

Women legislators worked for years to get a statue of Susan B. Anthony, Lucretia Mott, and Elizabeth Cady Stanton into the Capitol rotunda. In spring of 1977, they finally succeeded. At the dedication ceremony, Representative Louise Slaughter (D., NY) quipped to the statue, "Well sisters, it's going to be very hard to put you back in the basement now."

The Women's Bill of Rights

At the Seneca Falls suffragette convention on July 19, 1848, the Declaration of Independence was rewritten to include women, and a slew of resolutions were passed designed to promote gender equality. Among them were:

"Resolved, That all laws which prevent women from occupying such a station in society as her conscience shall dictate, or which place her in a position inferior to that of man, are contrary to the great precept of nature, and therefore of no force or authority.

"Resolved, That woman is man's equal—was intended to be so by the Creator, and the highest good of the race demands that she should be recognized as such.

"Resolved, That the women of this country ought to be enlightened in regard to the laws under which they live, that they may no longer publish their degradation by declaring themselves satisfied with their present position, nor their ignorance, by asserting that they have all the rights they want.

"Resolved, That it is the duty of the women of this country to secure themselves their sacred right to the elective franchise.

Resolved, that the equality of human rights results necessarily from the fact of the identity of the race in capacities and responsibilities.

Resolved, That...[these] being...self-evident truth[s] growing out of the divinely implanted principles of human nature, any custom or authority adverse to it, whether modern or wearing the hoary sanction of antiquity, is to be regarded as...self-evident falsehood, and at war with mankind."

ABOUT THE AUTHOR

Becca Anderson is an author, teacher, and writing instructor living in the San Francisco Bay Area. Originally from Ohio, Becca's background in women's studies has given her a lifelong passion for empowering women through their own herstory. The author of *The Book of Awesome Women*, Becca Anderson credits her first-grade teacher as a great inspiration. She runs several popular classes and workshops including "How to Put Your Passion on Paper." Anderson is currently at work on a book about women warriors from ancient and medieval times.

Mango Publishing, established in 2014, publishes an eclectic list of books by diverse authors—both new and established voices—on topics ranging from business, personal growth, women's empowerment, LGBTQ+ studies, health, and spirituality to history, popular culture, time management, decluttering, lifestyle, mental wellness, aging, and sustainable living. We were named 2019 *and* 2020's #1 fastest-growing independent publisher by *Publishers Weekly*. Our success is driven by our main goal, which is to publish high-quality books that will entertain readers as well as make a positive difference in their lives.

Our readers are our most important resource; we value your input, suggestions, and ideas. We'd love to hear from you—after all, we are publishing books for you!

Please stay in touch with us and follow us at:

Facebook: Mango Publishing
Twitter: @MangoPublishing
Instagram: @MangoPublishing
LinkedIn: Mango Publishing
Pinterest: Mango Publishing
Newsletter: mangopublishinggroup.com/newsletter

Join us on Mango's journey to reinvent publishing, one book at a time.